Finding Joy in Studying

from the same author

The Neurodiverse Workplace
An Employer's Guide to Managing and Working with Neurodivergent Employees, Clients and Customers
Victoria Honeybourne
ISBN 978 1 78775 033 3
eISBN 978 1 78775 034 0

The Neurodiverse Classroom
A Teacher's Guide to Individual Learning Needs and How to Meet Them
Victoria Honeybourne
ISBN 978 1 78592 362 3
eISBN 978 1 78450 703 9

of related interest

The Dyslexia, ADHD, and DCD-Friendly Study Skills Guide
Tips and Strategies for Success
Ann-Marie McNicholas
ISBN 978 1 78775 177 4
eISBN 978 1 78775 178 1

The Memory and Processing Guide for Neurodiverse Learners
Strategies for Success
Alison Patrick
Illustrated by Matt Patrick
ISBN 978 1 78775 072 2
eISBN 978 1 78775 073 9

Finding Joy in Studying

An Autistic and ADHD Guide to Uncovering the Study Skills that Work for You

Victoria Honeybourne

Illustrated by Victoria Barron

Jessica Kingsley Publishers
London and Philadelphia

First published in Great Britain in 2025 by Jessica Kingsley Publishers
An imprint of John Murray Press

1

Copyright © Victoria Honeybourne 2025

The right of Victoria Honeybourne to be identified as the Author of the Work has been asserted by her in accordance with the Copyright, Designs and Patents Act 1988.

Illustrations copyright © Victoria Barron 2025

All rights reserved. No part of this publication may be reproduced, stored in a retrieval system, or transmitted, in any form or by any means without the prior written permission of the publisher, nor be otherwise circulated in any form of binding or cover other than that in which it is published and without a similar condition being imposed on the subsequent purchaser.

All pages marked ★ may be downloaded for personal use with this program, but may not be reproduced for any other purposes without the permission of the publisher

The fonts, layout and overall design of this book have been prepared according to dyslexia friendly principles. At JKP we aim to make our books' content accessible to as many readers as possible.

A CIP catalogue record for this title is available from the British Library and the Library of Congress

ISBN 978 1 80501 253 5
eISBN 978 1 80501 254 2

Printed and bound in China by Leo Paper Products Ltd

Jessica Kingsley Publishers' policy is to use papers that are natural, renewable and recyclable products and made from wood grown in sustainable forests. The logging and manufacturing processes are expected to conform to the environmental regulations of the country of origin.

Jessica Kingsley Publishers
Carmelite House
50 Victoria Embankment
London EC4Y 0DZ

www.jkp.com

John Murray Press
Part of Hodder & Stoughton Limited
An Hachette UK Company

The authorised representative in the EEA is Hachette Ireland,
8 Castlecourt Centre, Dublin 15, D15 XTP3, Ireland (email: info@hbgi.ie)

Contents

1. Introduction 7
2. Understand Your "Why" 19
3. Understand Yourself – and Your Neurodivergence 41
4. Time Management, Focus and Organization 67
5. Reading and Note-Taking 115
6. Written Assignments 143
7. Presentation Skills 179
8. Revision and Exams 201

   Further Resources 237

   References 239

Chapter 1

INTRODUCTION

Welcome to *Finding Joy in Studying: An Autistic and ADHD Guide to Uncovering the Study Skills that Work for You!*

I've been *really* excited about writing this book! You see, I love studying. I'm happiest when I'm enrolled in some sort of course, when I'm learning something new and when I'm applying my new knowledge to writing assignments. Being autistic, I tend to study best in my own way (a way which often appears illogical to anybody observing!). I've worked with many neurodivergent students in schools and higher education and know that studying can be frustrating – often not because of any difficulty in understanding the subject matter but because our brains process things differently and learn in a different way to what's usually expected in education institutions.

I've learned how to be relatively successful studying, but my ways of studying might not be useful to anybody else, whether they're autistic, ADHD, neurotypical or whatever their neurotype. I've learned (and am still learning) how my brain works and I've gained the confidence to work with that, rather than against it. That's what this book is about. This isn't just a book of study hacks; it isn't a book of "do this, not that". Yes, you'll find many tips and strategies to try out and choose from, but more importantly you'll have the opportunity to learn and reflect on what works best for YOU, for YOUR unique neurodivergent brain. And that's really exciting, because it's something only you can discover! But, anyway, before we do a deep dive into all of that, this introduction will take you through what's meant by study skills, why they're so important and the coaching approach this book takes.

SO, WHAT ARE STUDY SKILLS?

Study skills are just that – the various skills needed to study effectively.

IMPORTANT

- This book is for you to use in whatever way works for you. Write lists, make mind maps, draw pictures, write poems … it really is completely up to you!

- Also, there aren't any right or wrong responses to any of the questions. Go with your gut feeling and don't worry if you can't answer every prompt. Not every question will be relevant to every individual. You might also find that you need time to reflect on the questions – insights might not come immediately. Try returning to some of the prompts in a few weeks or months and reflect on your experiences.

 Think about a recent essay or project you completed. What was it?

....

....

Now, can you break it down into all the small tasks you needed to do to complete it?

- ....
- ....
- ....
- ....
- ....

Let's say you used the example of writing an essay. The smaller tasks required might have included:

INTRODUCTION

I needed to...

- Understand what the question is asking
- Identify where to find the information
- Do any necessary reading or research
- Decide what to include in the essay
- Decide which order to put the information in
- Write up the essay in an appropriate academic style
- Proofread the essay for clarity
- Stay focused while working on the previous tasks
- And finally, submit the essay before the deadline!

These smaller steps are all examples of study skills.

Some others are included in this diagram:

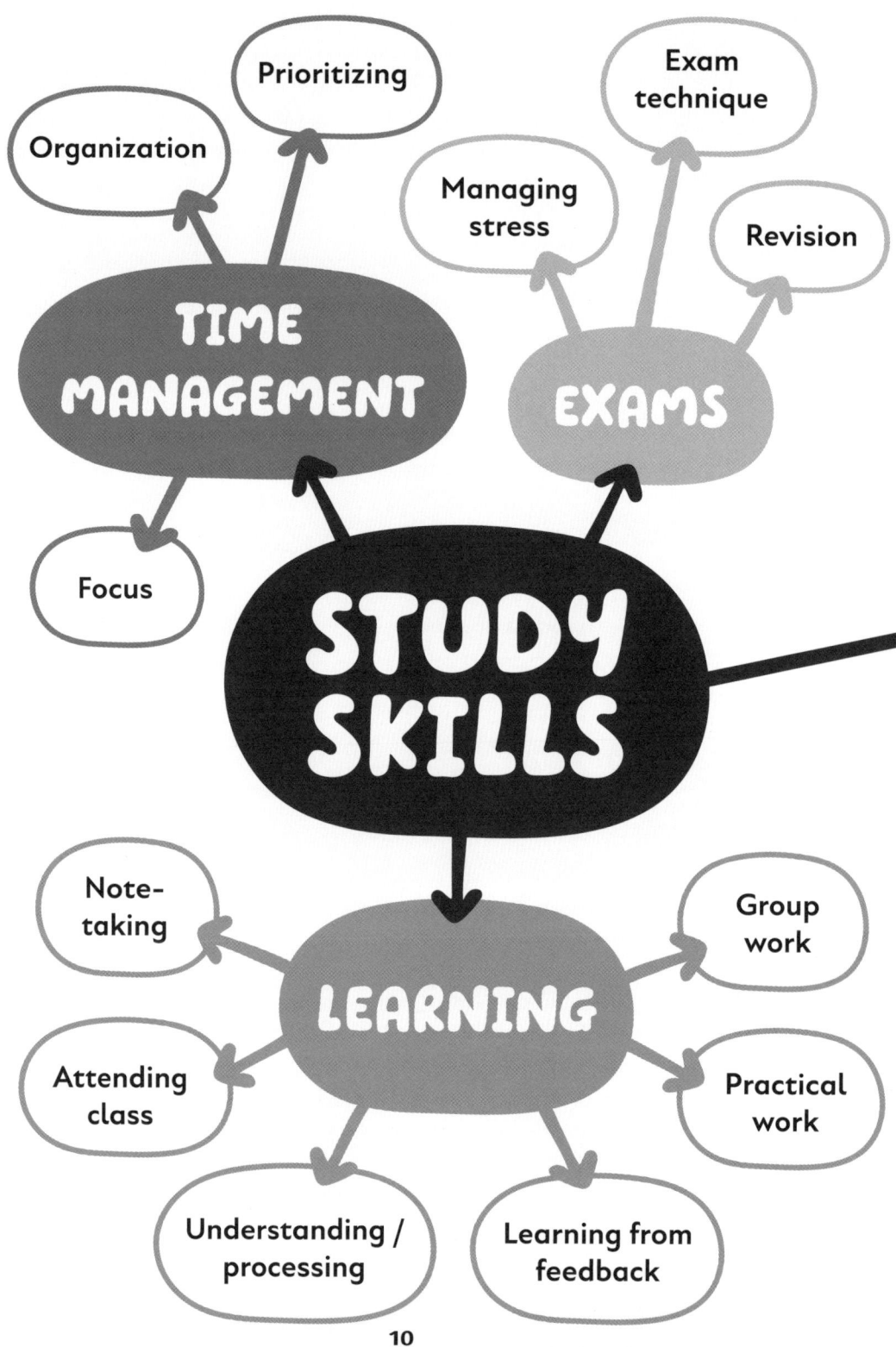

INTRODUCTION

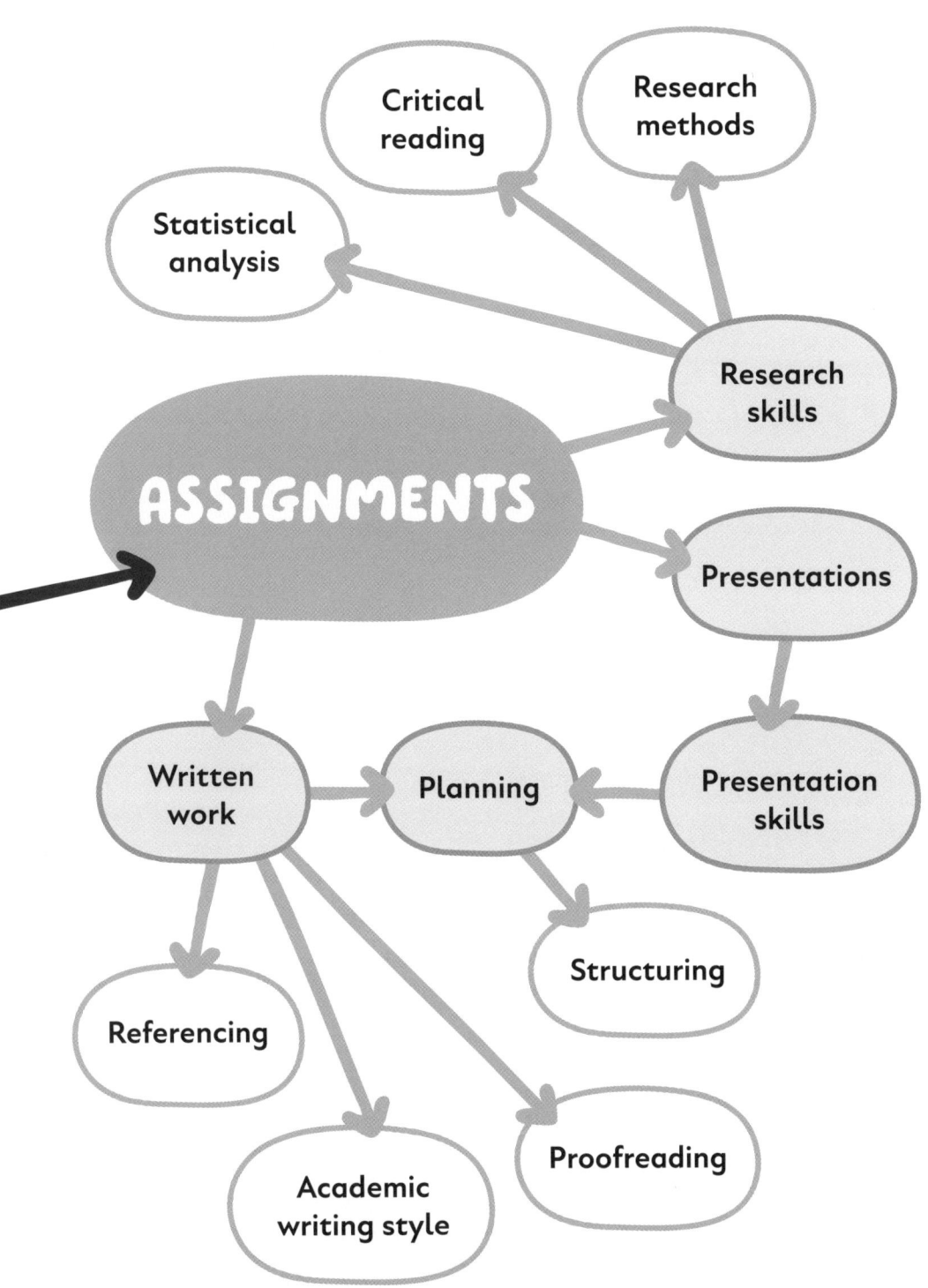

There might be some differences depending on the subject you're studying – some subjects rely more on practical assessments, for example – but study skills are more or less the same, whether you're studying arts, humanities, sciences or a work-related qualification.

AND WHY ARE THEY IMPORTANT?

Have you ever noticed some students who really seem to know what they're talking about in class aren't always those who do best in their assignments and exams? Or perhaps you've met somebody who seems really intelligent but just hasn't ever managed to complete a formal qualification? If you're reading this book, maybe you're one of those people yourself. Some individuals don't seem to do as well in assessments and examinations as they do in everyday life. They don't necessarily have difficulty with understanding the actual content, but rather they have less effective study skills – difficulties applying this knowledge in the way that's expected to achieve formal qualifications.

Effective study skills can make a huge difference not only to how well you do at studying, but also to how easy and enjoyable you find the process. If you can't manage your time effectively to get an assignment completed and submitted by the due date, then your grades aren't likely to reflect your true ability. You're also likely to feel more stressed and overwhelmed than if you were more organized.

Many people can find study skills difficult. Some have never been taught them explicitly. Others might never have found the strategies that work for them – the one-size-fits-all approach taken in many classrooms doesn't work for everyone, especially not for those who are neurodivergent. Being neurodivergent, you'll probably have differences with how you process information or with executive functioning skills (the skills needed to prioritize, organize yourself, get things started and finished and manage your time). Other neurodivergent traits (such as hyperfocus, lack of focus, overthinking, sensory issues or anxiety) can also affect studying, as well as other aspects of life.

INTRODUCTION

Study skills aren't only useful for formal education. Want to drive a car? Knowing how you can revise for a theory test and manage nerves during a practical test will be essential. Planning on becoming self-employed? Understanding how you work best, how to organize yourself and how to manage your time will be vital. Looking for advice about a financial, health, social or political issue? Being able to identify reliable and trustworthy sources of information in the era of information overload is key.

A note! This book isn't about trying to make "a square peg fit a round hole". As a neurodivergent individual myself, and as somebody who's spent a lot of time supporting neurodivergent students, I realize that assessment methods in education are not always very inclusive of different learning styles and that this really needs to change. This book is not about trying to get you to study in more "neurotypical ways". It's about helping you to learn effective study skills (ones that will work for your neurodivergent brain) that you can apply to all aspects of life – and that will help you meet the current requirements of the education system.

SPEAK UP AND FEED BACK!

Education systems and policies have traditionally been designed by neurotypicals for neurotypicals. Understanding and acceptance of neurodiversity has increased greatly over recent years, yet many educational institutions are still adapting to meeting the needs of neurodivergent students. The likelihood is, if you are struggling with an aspect of learning, then so are many others. Leaders, policy-makers and tutors need your help!

- Fill in module / course feedback forms and outline what changes you think need to be made for neurodivergent students.

- Speak to your college or university's disability service or school's SENCo (Special Educational Needs Co-ordinator) – they can act as an advocate or pass on feedback to teachers and tutors.

- Get involved with your setting's student council. More neurodivergent (and other minority) voices are needed!

WHO'S THIS BOOK FOR?

This book is designed for any student who identifies as neurodivergent, but especially those who identify as autistic and / or ADHD.

You might have a formal diagnosis, be awaiting a diagnosis, or just suspect you might be neurodivergent – it doesn't matter, this book is for you (and neurotypicals might find it useful too!).

WHAT IS NEURODIVERSITY?

Neurodiversity describes the diversity in the way human brains function. For a long time, it was believed that everybody's brain "worked" in the same way. Anybody who appeared to function differently (for example, having difficulties or differences that we would now associate with dyslexia, autism, ADHD or other conditions) was told that there was "something wrong with them", that they were deficient in some way and that they should learn to function more "normally".

Thankfully, attitudes towards neurodiversity are finally changing. It's now more recognized that brains function in a range of ways and that this is simply another aspect of human variation. So, whereas it was conventionally considered that there was one "right" or "normal" way to be and that other ways were inferior, there is now more acceptance that there are many different neurotypes – and that these are all equally valid, just different ways of being.

"Neurotypical" is the term given to those whose brains function in the way currently accepted as the dominant, most socially-accepted style, and "neurodivergent" covers people whose brains work differently to this (for example, those with diagnoses of autism / Asperger Syndrome, ADHD, dyslexia, dyspraxia, dyscalculia, dysgraphia, Tourette's or sensory processing disorders). Individuals can have more than one neurodivergent condition.

INTRODUCTION

A SUPER-QUICK GUIDE TO SOME NEURODIVERGENT CONDITIONS

ADHD
ADHD stands for Attention Deficit Hyperactivity Disorder. People who have a diagnosis of ADHD have difficulties with inattention and with hyperactivity and / or impulsivity which affect everyday life. Symptoms can change as a person gets older and it's believed that ADHD is underdiagnosed in females. It's thought up to 5% of children and up to 4% of adults are affected (ADHD UK, 2024).

Autism
Autism is a condition which affects social interaction and communication and which involves repetitive or restricted behaviours. Autistic people experience sensory sensitivities and many have highly-focused hobbies or interests and anxiety. The term Asperger Syndrome was used in the past to describe autistic people without learning difficulties and is sometimes still used today. It's thought over 1% of people are autistic and autism has been under-diagnosed in females (NAS, 2024).

Dyscalculia
Dyscalculia is a condition which affects the understanding of numbers and simple number concepts. It's thought about 6% of people have dyscalculia (BDA, 2024b).

Dyslexia
Dyslexia is a condition which affects reading and writing skills. Dyslexic people have difficulty processing and recalling information they see and hear. Dyslexia also affects skills such as coordination, memory and organization. Ten per cent of the population are thought to be affected by dyslexia (BDA, 2024a).

Dyspraxia
Dyspraxia (sometimes known as DCD – Developmental Coordination Disorder) affects movement, spatial awareness and coordination. It can also affect organization, attention, concentration and time management. It affects up to 6% of people (Foundation for People with Learning Disabilities, 2024).

> Do note that these are very brief definitions! Neurodivergent conditions are complex and can affect every part of a person's being. They also affect each and every individual differently. Look at the Further Resources list at the end of this book if you want to know where to find out more.

Of course, just because there is now more recognition of neurodiversity, that doesn't mean the world's suddenly become more neurodivergent-friendly. Current systems and societal expectations are often still based on the neurotypical style of functioning, and there can still be stereotypes, prejudice and negative attitudes demonstrated towards those who are neurodivergent. Hopefully, however, this will continue to improve for the better.

TERMINOLOGY

Just a note here about the language used in this book. The language used to describe neurodiversity has changed LOTS in recent years and continues to change as new perspectives and theories are discussed. I've used the terms considered most acceptable to the majority at the time of writing – for example, research (Kenny *et al.*, 2015) shows that generally autistic people prefer to be called "autistic people" as opposed to "people with autism" – but apologies in advance if you're reading this and preferred terminology has changed quicker than this book has been updated!

Also, the rapid introduction of AI and digital technologies in the education sector means that the way students are taught and assessed is rapidly changing. I focus in this book on general study skills that will remain relevant for the foreseeable future.

I've deliberately avoided, where possible, recommending specific technology or software, as that sort of information can become out-of-date even by the time the book goes to print! Check with your school, department, library service or Disability Advisor about any software currently recommended for your needs or subject.

INTRODUCTION

WHAT APPROACH DOES THIS BOOK TAKE?

Finding Joy in Studying uses a coaching approach. This isn't a book of advice, saying "Do this, then do that" – though there are useful tips and strategies for you to choose from throughout. Instead, it is a book which encourages you to find your own answers, helps you identify what your personal barriers are, and encourages you to find strategies that will work for you.

The book uses techniques from the field of coaching. You might have heard terms such as "life coaching", "health coaching" or "career coaching". The emphasis in a coaching approach, whatever aspect of life you are applying it to, is that you're considered the expert on your own life, not the professional who is helping. Many people find coaching approaches really helpful.

Coaching:

- uses questioning and supportive challenging to help you gain self-awareness
- encourages you to identify goals that are meaningful to you
- helps you to identify the barriers you face
- supports you to uncover any limiting beliefs that prevent you from reaching your goals
- puts you "in the driving seat"
- encourages increased self-awareness and personal growth
- helps you to learn rather than teaches you.

So, this book really is to help *you* get to know *you*. It's to empower you to take control of your studying, to help you identify your goals, your strengths, your limiting beliefs and exactly what support you need. There are practical strategies of how you can apply this knowledge to developing and improving effective study skills that work for you, and activities that will help you gain confidence in working in your own way.

All pages marked with ★ can be downloaded from www.jkp.com/catalogue/book/9781805012535.

SUMMARY

In this chapter you've learned:

- Study skills include a range of skills such as time management, research, note-taking writing and exam technique.

- Study skills are vital to doing well – and can help outside formal education situations too!

- Being neurodivergent can affect how you study due to differences in how you process and understand information and differences with executive functioning skills.

- A coaching approach sees you as the expert – your knowledge of how your brain works and what suits you is the key to improving your study skills.

- Educational institutions are not always as inclusive for different learning styles as they could be – speak to your SENCo or Disability Officer to pass on feedback.

Chapter 2
UNDERSTAND YOUR "WHY"

Think of something you're really motivated about – a hobby, interest, social issue, job or school subject perhaps.

Why do you feel so motivated about this? Note down your thoughts here:

....
....
....
....
....
....
....
....
....
....
....
....
....
....

FINDING JOY IN STUDYING

What did you identify from the prompt on the previous page? Maybe you realized you simply get a great deal of enjoyment or joy from engaging in the task. Perhaps you're motivated because of some sort of external reward – such as the pay from employment or achieving a qualification in order to be able to pursue your chosen career path. Or maybe your motivation comes from a deeper sense of purpose – there's something about the task that's meaningful to you on a deeper level. For example, you might take a reusable cup with you to college each day, as using less plastic and reducing your environmental footprint is something that's important to you.

Motivation is really important when it comes to studying. If you're feeling motivated, you're more likely to want to spend time studying and do extra work that is necessary. If you're feeling less motivated, studying can feel a hundred times harder. You probably won't put the time in, will prioritize other things and find it all feels like a lot of hard work.

Are there times you lack motivation?

....
....
....
....
....
....

Why do you think this is?

....
....
....
....
....
....

UNDERSTAND YOUR "WHY"

Did you have any insights from reflecting on your motivation zappers? When do you struggle to find motivation for a task? Is it when you find something boring or difficult? When you feel you "have" to do something, rather than "want" to do it? When something doesn't align with what's important to you? When you don't understand the reasoning behind something?

This chapter is all about finding your "why" – *Why* are you studying? *Why* is this important to you? *Why* do you want to do as well as you can? Getting clear about your reasons can help to increase motivation, keeping you focused on what you want to achieve. So, it's time to get you excited about what you're studying and why...

What do you love about your chosen subject? What do you find absolutely fascinating?

....
....
....
....

What have you enjoyed most about your studies so far? And / or what are you most looking forward to doing?

....
....
....
....

Why did you choose to study this subject or qualification?

....
....
....
....

Do you have longer-term goals? What do you want to do in the future and how will this subject / qualification help?

....
....
....
....

Why is this subject important to you? (Not to your family, friends, teachers or society in general, but why is it important and meaningful to you?)

....
....
....
....

> "I get to do a whole PhD around my special interest! It's been amazing!"

WORKING OUT WHAT'S MEANINGFUL TO YOU

You might have found it easy to recognize why your subject is important to you. If you weren't so sure, identifying your values might help give you more insight. Values are the things that are important to you, the principles that guide your actions and decisions. Environmental awareness, community, self-expression, wellbeing or justice are all examples of values (a longer list can be found in the next activity). People often feel happier and more comfortable when they are living in alignment with their personal values, and being aware of what your values are can help you make decisions that are right for you. This includes study-related decisions such as whether to

UNDERSTAND YOUR "WHY"

pursue further study or which subjects to focus on. Values can change over time as you gain more life experience, so it can be useful to reflect on your values at different points in your life.

 You could start by thinking about the following questions:

- What do you enjoy doing in your free time?

    ....
    ....
    ....
    ....

- What's most important to you in your life?

    ....
    ....
    ....
    ....

- What would your perfect day look like?

    ....
    ....
    ....
    ....

- When do you feel happiest / most content / most fulfilled?

    ....
    ....
    ....
    ....

FINDING JOY IN STUDYING

Do your answers suggest what's important to you?

....

....

....

....

You might find it easier to choose your top values from a "values list". Look at the list on the following page.

- Start by circling the words that resonate with you the most. Try to be selective so you don't end up with too many words.

- Add your own words in the blank boxes if there are other values that are more meaningful to you. You might choose to merge similar values into one group (e.g. "health", "wellbeing" and "physical fitness" might become "wellbeing") if that makes more sense to you.

UNDERSTAND YOUR "WHY"

Accomplishment	Health	Adventure	Ambition
Art	Awe	Belonging	Simplicity
Fitness	Challenge	Advocacy	Community
Creativity	Ethics	Wellbeing	Inclusivity
Fun	Enjoyment	Environment	Expertise
Individuality	Family	Freedom	Friendship
Making a difference	Generosity	Humour	Independence
Spirituality	Integrity	Social Equality	Knowledge
Emotional health	Nature	Wealth	Religion
Personal growth	Volunteering	Commitment	Connection
Risk-taking	Honesty	Joy	Recognition
Tolerance	Solitude	Security	Trust
Learning	Self-expression	Resilience	Justice

Next, try to narrow down your values so you're left with a few of your top values and write them below:

My top values are:

- ....
....
- ....
....
- ....
....
- ....
....

Consider the top values you've identified from these exercises. Do these relate to the studying you've chosen to do? There might be an obvious connection, for example your top value is caring and you're studying nursing, but links might also be less obvious. For example, you might identify "appreciating differences" as a top value and be studying English Literature because you enjoy experiencing other cultures and people through the written word. Knowing that your studying is meaningful to you can help you find ongoing purpose and motivation.

MOTIVATION MAKERS AND ZAPPERS

There are times you might feel more motivated to study than others. Consider what affects your motivation levels. You can think back to the start of the chapter if you need to.

> What really helps you feel motivated and inspired about studying? Perhaps for you it's discussing your subject with like-minded classmates, or maybe there's a blog, vlog, book or podcast about your subject that always reminds you how interesting you find it. List what helps lift your motivation levels. Come back to this list if you're ever feeling low on motivation.

MY MOTIVATION MAKERS

-
-
-
-
-
-
-

And does anything zap your motivation for studying? Perhaps it's when you feel overwhelmed by too many deadlines, when you feel you're not doing as well as you'd like, or when you have to study a topic that doesn't interest you so much. This awareness can be helpful. You might realize there's a particular issue you need to focus on (such as time management) or perhaps need to remind yourself to think about the bigger picture (e.g. "Okay, so I know I'm really not that interested in this topic, but it won't last forever, and some of the information will be necessary for the topics I am more interested in").

GETTING TO KNOW YOURSELF

Getting to know yourself can help you make choices that keep your motivation levels high. Some neurodivergent individuals, for example, have a need for "novelty". They get bored quickly and prefer to be learning new things and trying out new experiences. Having this knowledge about yourself can help you recognize why your motivation for something may have fallen and can help you make choices to reduce the impact of this. For example, you might choose optional modules from other subject areas or about unfamiliar topics to keep interest up, or you might choose to take part in work experience or other activities that allow you to apply your skills and knowledge in new and different ways, or might simply find that mixing up where and how you study helps.

Other neurodivergent individuals may dislike new experiences and prefer feelings of certainty and familiarity. Recognizing this can help you understand why you might be finding something more difficult. Some neurodivergent individuals might like new experiences at some times and prefer the same routine at other times. It doesn't really matter what your preferences are, it's the self-knowledge that's important. This book is about gaining that all-important self-insight. The activities will provide opportunities to reflect on different aspects of studying.

Note: You might also find it helpful to keep an on-going journal to track your thoughts and progress. And, if you need further support, you could try talking things through with a mentor, therapist or counsellor.

CREATE YOUR SPACE

The environment around you can really make a difference to how you feel and your motivation levels. You might not have much choice over where you attend lectures or classes (though do let your school or university know if the physical environment creates barriers to your learning due to your sensory issues) but you'll likely be able to choose where you complete your independent study – at home, in the library or with friends, for example. Creating a space that you love to be in can help you feel more motivated to study there and, if you have sensory sensitivities, can ensure you feel comfortable and able to concentrate.

Creating your study space

- **Lighting** – What works for you: a reading lamp, a well-lit area or soft twinkly lights?
- **Colour** – Do you have any choice over the colours in your study space? Colours can support the creation of different moods and atmospheres. Which colours create feelings of calm for you? Or do you prefer colours that help you feel energized?
- **Sound** – Do you prefer to study in silence? With quiet background music? With white noise? With noise-cancelling headphones in? With a general background hum of conversation?
- **Visuals** – Are there specific photos, pictures or items you like to surround yourself with?
- **Aroma** – Do you find certain smells calming or reassuring? Perhaps you like to use a diffuser, air freshener or scented candles? (Remember not to leave these unattended.)
- **Distractions** – Are you easily distracted? How can you limit distractions from the environment, other people or digital devices?
- **Clutter** – Keeping your study space clutter-free can improve organization as well as reduce feelings of overwhelm. Would you benefit from tidying your study area? Can you organize your resources effectively?

- **Physical comfort** – Adequate hydration is really important for concentration, mood and health. Do you remember to drink enough? And do you eat at regular intervals? What about your sitting posture? A supportive, comfortable chair at the right height can make a difference, as can getting up for a walk or stretch at regular intervals. Taking breaks to look away from the screen is also a good idea, as well as ensuring the screen is at a suitable height to avoid neck strain.

If you're studying in a library or public space you might be limited in what you can do – but do try and seek out a space that meets your needs. If you're at home you might have more influence over your study space.

Time to get creative! Design your ideal study space here. What could you realistically do to make it a space you look forward to spending time in?

WELLBEING

Motivation levels for studying can also be affected by your wider level of wellbeing. When you're ill, for example, or feeling lonely, depressed, anxious or stressed, it's likely you might find it harder to feel as motivated as you usually do.

If you're struggling with your wellbeing, do seek support as soon as you can. This might be from your GP, your school or university's Student Services / Wellbeing Service, a counsellor or therapist, a mentor, or from a charity that offers face-to-face, telephone or online support.

Note down here the support that is available to you. There might be services you've accessed before, or you might want to look at what's available at your school or university:

....
....
....

What else contributes to a good level of wellbeing for you? Do you feel better when you take regular exercise? When you spend time with good friends? When you engage with hobbies you enjoy? When you spend time outdoors?

....
....
....
....
....

UNDERSTAND YOUR "WHY"

 My wellbeing boosters are:

MY WELLBEING BOOSTERS

-
-
-
-
-
-
-
-

FINDING JOY IN STUDYING

 How could you ensure you do some of these things on a regular basis? Could you set reminders for yourself? Sign up in advance to the activities you enjoy? Schedule a regular meet-up time with friends?

....
....
....
....
....
....
....
....
....
....
....
....
....
....
....
....
....
....
....
....

OTHER HEALTH ISSUES

If you have a health condition alongside your neurodivergent condition, you might encounter additional challenges when studying.

Some research is beginning to suggest that neurodivergent individuals might be more likely to experience long-term health conditions than their neurotypical counterparts, especially conditions such as Ehlers-Danlos Syndrome, joint hypermobility, pain conditions and gastrointestinal conditions (Donaghy et al., 2023), as well as pre-menstrual syndrome (PMS) and pre-menstrual dysphoric disorder (PMDD; Obaydi & Puri, 2008). If you're affected by a health condition, do remember to factor this in when working through this book, especially when considering issues such as time management and concentration, as these can be affected by fatigue, brain fog, pain and other symptoms. Do seek support for other issues too and speak to your health professional about ways of managing any other conditions.

CULTIVATE CURIOSITY

Getting curious (non-judgementally) about yourself, your studying and life in general is something that can help your wellbeing and ability to cope with different situations.

Imagine thinking:

> Today's class is going to be really boring.

You've already decided it's going to be boring. You're probably not looking forward to it and wishing you were doing something else. Perhaps you're wondering if you should skip class as there'll be no point in attending if you're going to be so bored. You go to class believing it's going to be boring, so perhaps you don't give it your full attention or you get your laptop out and start scrolling social media instead of taking notes. See how one thought alters your mindset and behaviour?

Now imagine thinking instead:

> **I wonder what today's class will be like?**

You're curious about what it will be like. You're not making any judgement in advance. You probably feel okay about attending, and turn up feeling open-minded, curious and in a better frame of mind. Of course, it's no guarantee the class will be the most exciting ever, but you've given it a chance and will probably gain more from attending than had you gone in telling yourself it was going to be the most boring hour you'll ever experience.

How can you cultivate a little more curiosity in life? Are there any thoughts or beliefs you could reframe from a place of curiosity? Write down your thoughts in the table below and how you can reframe them.

Current thought	From a place of curiosity
I won't fit in at the debating club.	I wonder what the debating club will be like? I'll go and see.

UNDERSTAND YOUR "WHY"

IT'S NOT ONLY THE ACADEMIC WORK

There's a well-known saying that "life is about the journey, not the destination". It's great to have one eye on your end goal (perhaps the job or lifestyle you want in the future) but don't forget to enjoy the studying journey. Whether you're at school, college, university or studying part-time or through distance learning, remember to enjoy the process – it's a great opportunity to immerse yourself in subjects and topics that you find fascinating and develop numerous skills and abilities along the way. There's often a social aspect to studying too – it can be a great chance to meet like-minded friends and get involved with clubs and societies.

Note down here any non-academic aspects of student life you enjoy. Or is there anything you don't already do but would like to get involved in? (An extra-curricular club, a society, the student council, being a course representative...) How could you go about getting involved in this?

....
....
....
....
....
....
....
....
....

BE YOUR OWN CHEERLEADER

 Write down five positive affirmations or words of encouragement to yourself.

UNDERSTAND YOUR "WHY"

Remind yourself of these when you need a boost – perhaps you could display them around your workspace or put them somewhere you'll see them regularly if you think that would help. Here are some of mine if you're struggling to think of your own.

SUMMARY

In this chapter, you've looked at identifying your "why" – the reasons why you are studying and why they are important to you. Being aware of your "why" can aid motivation and keep you going when things are feeling tough. You've also considered what affects your motivation, considered your physical environment and thought about your wider wellbeing.

FINDING JOY IN STUDYING

 Summarize your thoughts here:

Things that keep my motivation levels topped up are...

. . . .

. . . .

. . . .

I'm really excited by my subject and my studies because...

. . . .

. . . .

. . . .

Come back to this page to remind yourself of your reasons next time you need an extra dose of motivation!

Chapter 3

UNDERSTAND YOURSELF – AND YOUR NEURODIVERGENCE

This chapter explores your:

- strengths
- skills
- achievements
- current situation
- neurodivergence.

Why are these relevant to study skills? Well, knowing yourself, or becoming more self-aware, is a key aspect of a coaching approach. Being aware of what you're already good at and what you're doing well can help you put those strengths to good use.

Understanding your current situation and challenges accurately and non-judgementally can help you become clear about exactly what you can and can't change, and can help reduce feelings of overwhelm.

And understanding how your neurodivergent brain operates is essential to ensuring that you work most effectively and that any support you receive is going to work for you. So, let's get started...

SKILLS, STRENGTHS AND ACHIEVEMENTS

Let's begin by considering your skills and strengths. Have you ever heard the expression "play to your strengths"?

It's about knowing what you do well and then using that to your advantage. This can be applied to studying just like anything else. Knowing your strengths can help you choose to study in ways that suit you best. It's not about ignoring what you find more difficult or need to improve, but rather about using your strengths effectively to make progress in those more challenging areas.

Skills

First, consider your skills. A skill is the ability to do something. You've been gathering skills your whole life, in many cases probably without even realizing it.

List the skills you have. You could include:

- practical skills (the ability to play a musical instrument or use specific software effectively…)
- skills developed in education (research skills, writing or reading skills…)
- skills developed in the workplace (customer service skills, food hygiene, window dressing…)
- skills developed through voluntary work or community engagement (fundraising, sharing knowledge, advertising an event…)
- skills developed through hobbies and interests (football coaching skills, organizational skills…)
- skills developed in your personal life (caring responsibilities, advocacy skills…)
- transferable skills (communication skills, problem-solving skills…).

UNDERSTAND YOURSELF – AND YOUR NEURODIVERGENCE

 Some of my top skills are...

MY TOP SKILLS ARE:

-
-
-
-
-
-
-
-

> Go you!
> That's amazing!

Strengths

> "I get involved with the student council and am not afraid to speak up and advocate on behalf of other neurodivergent and disabled students."

Next, let's identify your strengths. Consider strengths across all aspects of life (you're going to consider strengths specifically related to studying a little later).

Take a look at this list of "strengths". Which do you think are your strengths? Use your own words in your list if there are other words that better describe your strengths.

Compassion	Kindness	Generosity	Humility
Humour	Creativity	Curiosity	Love of learning
Courage	Advocacy	Sense of justice	Standing up for your beliefs
Honesty	Spiritual awareness	Loyalty	Open-mindedness
Social intelligence	Emotional intelligence	Forgiveness	Gratitude
Optimism	Determination	Perseverance	Enthusiasm
Energy	Taking in new information	Critical thinking	Seeing multiple perspectives
Inclusive	Communication	Teamwork	Independence
Taking on new challenges	Caring	Carefulness	Non-judgemental
Musicality	Linguistic	Accuracy	Practical

UNDERSTAND YOURSELF – AND YOUR NEURODIVERGENCE

 My top strengths are...

MY TOP STRENGTHS ARE:

-
-
-
-
-
-
-
-

Great work! You're incredible!

Achievements

Now consider your achievements. It's likely you've achieved far more than you think. Achievements don't have to be major events that come with a certificate or trophy, they're anything you feel proud of, anything you've made happen or improved at or worked hard at. Examples could include: raising money for a charity, taking regular exercise, decorating a room to reflect the style you wanted, growing your own vegetables, performing at an event, learning how to drive, developing a more positive attitude towards something, persevering with a challenge, repairing a friendship...

Some achievements I'm most proud of are...

....
....
....
....

> Well done! Great job!

Neurodivergence

> "I know I leave things to the last minute, but that means I have become good at taking in a lot of information quickly!"

Consider also if you've developed any skills or strengths as a direct result of being neurodivergent. For example, perhaps you've had to problem solve to overcome difficulties, perhaps a diagnosis has led to increased self-awareness, or maybe you've developed effective advocacy skills.

UNDERSTAND YOURSELF – AND YOUR NEURODIVERGENCE

STUDYING

So, you've thought about your strengths, skills and achievements in general, and many of these will influence how you study and your attitude towards studying. Now it's time to investigate how you study in more detail.

Looking over your answers to the previous questions, can you identify any skills or strengths which you could put to good use in your studying?

Studying strengths

What do you consider your strengths when it comes to studying? Write down your initial thoughts.

....
....
....
....
....
....
....
....

You might have found it easy to identify your studying strengths. If not, you might find the following audit helpful.

Study skills audit

Work through the following audit of study skills. Be honest with yourself about what you do well and what you find harder.

- Not every skill will be relevant to every subject. Also, this isn't an exhaustive list of study skills and you might like to add your own if there are skills more relevant to your specific course of study.

FINDING JOY IN STUDYING

STUDY SKILLS	I find this difficult	I am okay with this	I generally do this well
In class			
I attend classes (seminars/lectures/practical sessions etc.) regularly			
I am able to understand the information presented in class			
I take effective notes in class			
I stay on task and focus in class			
I ask when there's something I don't understand			
I contribute in class			
I carry out practical tasks accurately and competently			
Organization			
I know what assignments, exams and deadlines are approaching			
I organize my notes and resources effectively			
I hand in assignments on time			
I manage my time well, not leaving tasks until the last minute			
I prioritize the most important tasks			

Continued on next page.

UNDERSTAND YOURSELF – AND YOUR NEURODIVERGENCE

STUDY SKILLS		I find this difficult	I am okay with this	I generally do this well
Research	I know where, and how, to find relevant research and resources			
	I make notes effectively when researching a topic			
	I take effective notes in class			
	I focus and concentrate when working independently			
	I work with others effectively			
Completing assignments	I understand the meaning of assignment language (e.g. explain, describe, evaluate, analyse…)			
	I plan and structure my assignments well			
	I keep my answers relevant			
	I have effective oral presentation skills			
	I write in a suitable academic style			
	I present arguments in my own words			
	My sentences are clear and coherent			

Continued on next page.

STUDY SKILLS	I find this difficult	I am okay with this	I generally do this well
Assignments, cont.			
I have a clear argument linking paragraphs together effectively			
I proofread my work for correct spelling, punctuation and grammar			
I reference sources accurately			
Support			
I respond well to constructive criticism from tutors/peers			
I use the feedback from tutors to improve my assignments			
I know where to seek support if I am finding an aspect of studying difficult			
Exams and revision			
I prioritize which topics I need to revise and focus on			
I use revision strategies to prepare			
I manage exam stress effectively			
I manage my time well during exams			

From this exercise, you'll have gained an insight into your study skills profile. Knowing what you already do well and identifying what you find difficult can be really useful. You'll now know which chapters of this book to focus on and how to utilize any support you're entitled to most effectively.

UNDERSTAND YOURSELF – AND YOUR NEURODIVERGENCE

You might also want to consider *how* you completed the audit above. Try to reflect objectively. Were you too hard on yourself? Did you compare yourself to others rather than focusing on yourself? Did you find it more difficult to acknowledge your weaknesses or your strengths? Did you find it difficult to engage in self-reflection?

YOUR STUDY HABITS

The following exercises invite you to reflect on your study habits, allowing you to identify what works for you and what does not.

Tick your preferred answer.

How do you study best?

☐ I prefer to study in short blocks of time (e.g. 15–30 minute blocks here and there).

☐ I need longer blocks of uninterrupted study time.

☐ Other:

....
....
....

How do you work best?

☐ I can have multiple assignments on the go at the same time.

☐ I need to complete one assignment before I can turn my thoughts to another topic or subject.

☐ Other:

....
....
....

When do you study best?

☐ Early mornings

☐ Daytime

☐ Evenings

☐ Anytime

☐ It depends

Where do you study best?

☐ At home – alone

☐ At home – in a communal area

☐ In a library / study area – alone

☐ In a library / study area – with friends or classmates

☐ A public place (e.g. coffee shop)

☐ Anywhere

Make a note of your preferences and use these when planning your studying. If you know that you feel too tired to study effectively in the evenings, for example, schedule it for earlier in the day. If you find it difficult to switch between topics, try to organize your time to complete one assignment before you need to move on to the next.

UNDERSTAND YOURSELF – AND YOUR NEURODIVERGENCE

ABOUT YOUR NEURODIVERGENCE

Time to turn now to what being neurodivergent means to you, and how this affects your study skills.

What's your attitude to being neurodivergent? Do you see it positively, negatively, or something in between?

....

....

Why do you think this is?

....

....

....

....

....

Your attitude to your neurodivergence might influence various aspects of life. For example, if you embrace being neurodivergent and learn to work to your strengths, you might be more likely to have improved wellbeing than if you have a negative attitude towards yourself. Autistic burnout is more likely in autistic individuals who try to suppress or camouflage their autism (Attwood and Garnett, 2022). If you feel you need help understanding and accepting your neurodivergence, seek support from a specialist service – your school or university might be able to point you in the right direction if you don't know of any services near you.

Do you think you have any strengths as a direct result of being neurodivergent? Some neurodivergent individuals identify strengths such as those listed below, but yours might be different.

- Ability to focus for long periods on topics of interest (hyperfocus)
- Good attention to detail

- A logical approach
- Energy and enthusiasm for new ideas
- Ability to remember and recall
- A good visual memory
- Ability to work independently
- Ability to take in complex information
- Ability to make new and unique links
- Perseverance
- Determination
- Ability to identify new ways to complete tasks
- Able to ask for help

UNDERSTAND YOURSELF – AND YOUR NEURODIVERGENCE

 My strengths related to my neurodivergence are:

> "I've learned to have confidence in my own way of doing things. As a mature student I'm more confident to let tutors know I approach things in a different way to what's expected but I know I'll get it done that way."

FINDING JOY IN STUDYING

Do you feel you experience any difficulties as a direct result of being neurodivergent? Some common difficulties for neurodivergent students are listed below, but, again, yours might be different:

- group work
- communication with staff or peers
- working better in your own way
- organization
- time management
- staying focused
- focusing on one small detail or topic too much (hyperfocus)
- needing to complete a task before moving on to the next
- seeing "the big picture"
- processing auditory information
- making notes while listening
- needing processing time before contributing or answering
- feeling overwhelmed with too much information
- understanding what the question is asking
- reading "between the lines"
- going "off on a tangent" in your answers
- not wanting to appear different / ask for help
- sensory issues that affect focus and concentration
- anxiety
- perfectionism
- perceiving instructions and expectations as "demands"
- feeling sensitive to perceived criticism or rejection.

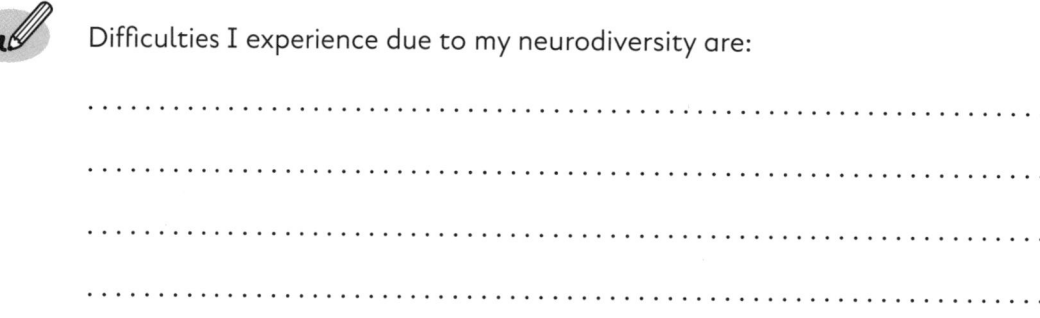

Difficulties I experience due to my neurodiversity are:

....

....

....

....

....

AUTISTIC / ADHD BURNOUT

You might have heard the terms "autistic burnout" or "ADHD burnout". These aren't official medical diagnoses but are terms often used by neurodivergent individuals to describe a long-term state of fatigue they experience as a result of their neurodivergence. Individuals describe experiencing symptoms such as:

- chronic extreme exhaustion
- a reduced ability to function how they usually do
- an increased sensitivity to sensory input
- mental exhaustion
- being unable to think clearly
- finding it hard to make decisions
- wanting to avoid social contact
- more frequent meltdowns or shutdowns
- losing the ability to "mask" ("masking" refers to autistic people attempting to appear more non-autistic – these might be conscious or unconscious)
- increased difficulties with executive functioning skills.

Autistic and ADHD burnout have only recently been researched in depth. A recent definition of autistic burnout offered by the National Autistic Society is:

> **Autistic burnout is a syndrome** conceptualised as resulting from chronic life stress and a mismatch of expectations and abilities without adequate supports. It is characterised by pervasive, long-term (typically 3+ months) exhaustion, loss of function, and reduced tolerance to stimulus. (NAS, 2022)

If you're experiencing autistic burnout it'll be affecting your studying as well as other aspects of your life. It'll help to seek support from a counsellor, therapist, mentor or other health professional with experience of supporting neurodivergent individuals. Many people experiencing autistic or ADHD burnout find that it helps their recovery to accept more support during this time, take care of their mental and physical health, and to advocate (or have someone advocate on their behalf) for greater understanding and acceptance of their neurodivergent needs.

What additional support, if any, do you currently get with your studies?

....
....
....
....

How useful is the support you receive? What would make it more helpful?

....
....
....
....

FIND OUT WHAT SUPPORT IS AVAILABLE

Disabled students, including those with a neurodivergent condition or mental health condition, can be eligible for extra support in education. If you're at school or college, you'll usually need to speak to the SENCo (Special Educational Needs Co-ordinator) who can tell you what support is available and what you're eligible for. If you're studying at a university, speak to your university's Disability Advisor, who can give you further information. If you don't already get additional support and are struggling, you'll usually be assessed by a Needs Assessor who will then advise on what type of support is most appropriate.

Examples of support that students might receive are:

UNDERSTAND YOURSELF – AND YOUR NEURODIVERGENCE

- extra time in exams or assessments
- extended deadlines
- being able to take exams in a separate room
- rest breaks during exams or assessments
- being able to dictate rather than handwrite answers in exams (using a scribe or voice-text software)
- using a reader (or screen-reader) to read questions aloud
- having one-to-one support in class or lectures
- specialist equipment or assistive technology
- one-to-one sessions with a specialist mentor or a study skills specialist
- digital devices (e.g. laptops) to run specialist software.

What you're eligible for will depend on your individual needs and circumstances.

> Don't forget also to look at the support that is available to all students. There might be much more than you realize. Most colleges and universities have a counselling or wellbeing service for all students to access. University librarians are on hand to support with research and information-finding skills. Student services departments might offer advice or run workshops on various aspects of academic and student life, and course tutors are available for subject-related queries.

Take some time to research and identify the support on offer at your college or university.

I've discovered my college / university offers:

....

....

....

....

ASKING FOR HELP

> "I got anxious about having conversations with tutors about how I need things done differently but it's definitely been worth it."

How comfortable do you feel asking for help when you need it?

....
....
....
....

If you're less confident, why do you think this is?

....
....
....
....
....

It can feel difficult asking for help, whatever your neurotype. Some people worry that they'll appear "stupid" or be laughed at, even though they know rationally that this is unlikely. It can be easy to compare yourself to peers who appear to "get it" and not need any extra support.

In reality though, there are many people who experience difficulties, and asking for help – though it can seem scary – is often the best way to get the support you need and can help you avoid many days, weeks or months of worry and anxiety over what you're struggling with.

UNDERSTAND YOURSELF – AND YOUR NEURODIVERGENCE

> "Having a specialist mentor has really helped me to navigate university life."

For neurodivergent individuals, there can be additional difficulties asking for help – perhaps social anxiety makes approaching tutors feel impossible, or maybe you've experienced negative reactions in the past when you've felt misunderstood or unsupported. If you struggle, consider what could help. Perhaps you could email your tutor instead of approaching them face-to-face? Maybe your Disability Advisor can act as an advocate for you? Perhaps listing and remembering the times you have asked for help successfully can help you feel more confident.

Note down any ideas about what could help:

....
....
....
....
....

LIMITING BELIEFS

Managing limiting beliefs is discussed in more detail in Chapter 8, but now's a good time to introduce the concept. A limiting belief is a (not necessarily true!) belief you have that stops you from moving forwards. Do you hold any limiting beliefs about your ability to study and learn? For example, you might believe "I'm no good at maths" and this belief might stop you from applying for a job that involves some work with numbers. If you challenge this belief, however, you might realize that it isn't as accurate as you believe. Perhaps it isn't that you're "no good at maths" but that you had a teacher who didn't explain the subject in a way that made sense to you, or that you simply did better at other subjects or felt you had to work harder than your classmates. (Just a note – comparing yourself to others is never helpful!) Limiting beliefs can be repeated so many times in our thoughts and speech that sometimes we start to believe them, even if they're objectively untrue.

Examples of limiting beliefs relating to studying can include:

- I never remember anything important.
- I'm no good at x/y/z.
- I'm not as clever as others.
- I can't do well in exams.
- I never get things done.
- I can't give presentations.
- I always make a fool of myself in class.
- People will think I'm stupid if I… (say I don't understand/ask for help).
- If I need extra help, I'm a failure.
- If I don't get 100%, I'm no good at this.
- I am autistic / dyslexic / ADHD so I'll never do well.

Do you recognize any limiting beliefs of your own?

Now, can you challenge any of these limiting beliefs to make them more accurate? Look for evidence which disproves your beliefs. For example, "I'm no good at maths" might become "I didn't understand topics like trigonometry the way they were explained at school, but I am good at managing my money and using numbers in everyday life, so that proves I have some good mathematical abilities".

Or "I can't do well in exams" might become "I haven't done as well as I'd like in school exams, but I did pass my driving theory test first time, so I can do well in exams". We'll delve further into limiting beliefs as you work through this book.

UNDERSTAND YOURSELF – AND YOUR NEURODIVERGENCE

For now, try to notice any that you experience and reframe them more accurately.

Try and disprove your beliefs here.

Current belief:

....

....

How I could reframe it:

....

....

Repeat this exercise with other limiting beliefs you have.

SUMMARY

In this chapter you've considered your strengths, skills and neurodivergence. You've identified your current study habits, the aspects of studying you're already doing well, the aspects you want to develop, and how your neurodivergence affects your studying. Use the following to summarize:

What do you already do well when studying?

....

....

....

....

....

Great job!

What difficulties do you currently face?

....
....
....
....
....

What areas do you want to develop? How would you like your current situation to change?

....
....
....
....
....

How will this make you feel? (For example, "I want to manage my time better so I'm handing in assignments on time. I'll feel on top of things rather than feeling stressed, which means I have to rush my work and don't feel it's a true reflection of my ability.")

....
....
....
....
....

Go you! You can do this!

UNDERSTAND YOURSELF – AND YOUR NEURODIVERGENCE

Do you need any support from your college or university? Write down any actions you are going to take here:

- ....
- ....
- ....

> Could you action any of these right now? If so, do them! Send the email or sign up for the workshop or confirm the needs assessment or whatever it is. Do it *right this minute* while it's at the front of your mind, before you put it off and it becomes another niggle on your to-do list. If you can't do it right now, set yourself an alarm or reminder to do it at the earliest point you can, or ask somebody to help you with it.

Chapter 4

TIME MANAGEMENT, FOCUS AND ORGANIZATION

In the earlier years of school, your time is mostly managed for you. Your week was probably timetabled with classes to attend. As you've moved through school, you've likely found you've received more homework tasks to do in your "free time". And the further you go with studying, the more independent study you're expected to do. Towards the end of secondary education there'll be exams which you're expected to revise for in your own time, as well as coursework assignments you have to prepare. In Higher Education, there's even more emphasis on independent study. You might have far fewer classes and lectures to attend than you're used to (also called less "contact time"). The rest of the time you're expected to study independently. This change can be difficult for many students who aren't used to it. Outside of classes and lectures you might be expected to complete tasks such as the following:

- read about a topic in preparation for a seminar
- complete group projects
- complete assignments such as presentations, reports, projects or essays
- revise for exams and assessments
- carry out research projects
- read "around your subject" – you'll usually be given a reading list for each module which suggests useful texts to choose from. Reading

around your subject gives you the in-depth knowledge required for understanding and assessments

- re-read and organize your lecture notes
- carry out practical work or get involved in extra-curricular activities (e.g. instrumental practice for Music students, lab work for Science students, conversation groups for students of Modern Foreign Languages).

So, good time management skills are essential to doing well at studying, particularly when studying at higher levels. Being unable to manage your time can quickly lead to you falling behind with your studying and finding your workload overwhelming. It can also lead to you not doing as well in assignments as you could.

Time management, organization and focus are considered together in this chapter as they can be closely linked. If you're disorganized, for example, you might waste time trying to find your resources, which will affect your time management. If you tend to hyperfocus on a small detail, you might find this leaves you with little time to complete the main part of a task.

Some of the most common difficulties and differences for neurodivergent students relating to these areas are explained in more detail below. Consider which apply to you.

> "I get a week's extension automatically for every assignment because of my disability, but I just see this as the deadline rather than the original date and still leave everything to the last minute."

EXECUTIVE FUNCTIONING SKILLS

Difficulties with **executive functioning skills** are often associated with neurodivergent conditions such as ADHD and autism. Executive functioning skills are the skills that help people complete everyday tasks and include planning, organizing, time management, working memory, attention, self-control, flexibility and perseverance. Some of the most common difficulties and differences are explained in more detail below; consider if any apply to you.

Time blindness

A common trait associated with ADHD can be the idea of **time blindness**, or differences in how the passing of time is perceived. One analogy used is that of seeing a ship on the horizon. Whereas somebody else would see the ship (the deadline) approaching slowly from a distance, somebody who experiences time blindness might not be aware of the ship until it's right in the harbour (e.g. the day the essay is due!). This might mean you:

- underestimate or overestimate how long a task will take
- feel a deadline is a "long way off" until it actually arrives and then feel "taken by surprise" by it
- lose track of time
- miss deadlines
- arrive late to appointments
- have difficulty keeping to a schedule.

Focus

Difficulties with focusing are also associated with ADHD (the **"attention deficit"** of Attention Deficit Hyperactivity Disorder). If you experience this, you might:

- be easily distracted by external distractions
- daydream or "zone out" frequently, including in conversations without realizing it
- lose your train of thought easily

- have multiple trains of thought going on simultaneously
- have difficulty paying attention when reading or listening
- find you switch from one task to another frequently
- start tasks and then lose interest
- become bored easily
- find it hard to distinguish between the relevant and irrelevant
- have difficulty completing tasks, especially those that are "boring" or "mundane"
- overlook details
- have difficulty remembering details
- work better on tasks that are more stimulating or that have instant rewards.

Hyperfocus

However, some neurodivergent individuals can become so engrossed and absorbed by a task that it is difficult for them to shift their attention. This is called **hyperfocus**. People who hyperfocus might become almost oblivious to anything else going on around them and ignore other everyday tasks that need to be done. Hyperfocus when studying can be a positive if you're focused on a study-related task, although it's also important to become aware of any downsides. Are you, for example, still getting other necessary everyday tasks done? And are you keeping on top of your studying as a whole, and not just the one topic you are hyperfocused on?

Shifting attention

Some neurodivergent individuals have difficulties with **shifting attention**. For example, some need to complete a task before they can move on to the next. Anything unfinished can feel like an "open tab", something which takes energy and concentration away from the task they've moved on to.

You can think of it like having multiple tabs open on a computer – too many can cause the whole system to slow down or fail to function effectively. Some neurodivergent individuals can feel like this – that too many unfinished tasks or unmade decisions can almost "freeze" them, making it hard to concentrate on other tasks.

Autistic / ADHD inertia

You might have heard the terms "autistic inertia" or "ADHD inertia". These are terms that some neurodivergent individuals use to describe their difficulties starting tasks, finishing tasks or switching between them. This phenomenon has only recently begun to be researched in detail.

You and other neurodivergent individuals might experience this inertia in different ways. There can be the difficulties already discussed:

- getting started on tasks (even if the task is something you want to do), shifting attention
- hyperfocusing and not being able to stop once started.

You can also experience:

- overwhelming indecision
- anxiety
- perfectionism when trying to plan or start tasks
- difficulties going back to a task after an interruption
- a lack of motivation
- lacking a sense of urgency about completing a task.

The thing that most people agree on is that the sense of inertia is **overwhelming** – their brain simply won't let them get started, even if it's a task they really want to do.

This might sound quite debilitating, but knowing it is common amongst neurodivergent individuals can help you accept it and realize that you're not just "being lazy" or "not trying hard enough". Some strategies that can support this inertia are covered in this chapter – there's no single solution that will work for everyone. It's all about getting to know how you experience inertia and what might work for you.

Other differences

Other traits can also affect focus and time management. The traits outlined below are, of course, found in the general population too, but are often particularly associated with neurodivergent conditions and can affect neurodivergent individuals to a greater degree, having a greater negative impact on their lives, especially in combination with their other neurodivergent differences.

Perfectionism

Having perfectionist traits might mean you spend too much time trying to get one small part of a task "perfect", leaving no time to complete the rest. Or you might not even attempt a task you don't think you'll be able to complete perfectly.

Overthinking

You might spend a long time worrying excessively about a task or situation, spending time thinking and worrying rather than actually completing the task.

Difficulty getting started

You find the hardest part of a task is getting started but work well once you've started. The task might seem overwhelming or too difficult.

Anxiety

Anxiety can manifest itself differently for different individuals and often impacts on concentration, focus and motivation.

Procrastination

Procrastination is when you delay or avoid a task, despite knowing that this could lead to negative consequences. There can be many reasons for procrastinating: a task seeming too difficult or too big; lacking confidence in your ability to complete a task; wanting to do something more enjoyable; being "stuck" on some aspect of a task; difficulty making a decision; or being worried about perceived criticism or rejection.

Demand avoidance

Some neurodivergent individuals perceive deadlines and study expectations as "demands", which causes overwhelming anxiety for them and leads to

TIME MANAGEMENT, FOCUS AND ORGANIZATION

them being unable to complete the task in question, even if it's something they enjoy or are usually capable of. (If you are affected to an extreme extent, this might be diagnosed as Pathological Demand Avoidance.)

Free time vs study time
A further difficulty you might have is the need to keep "studying" separate from "free time". This can cause difficulties with independent study or homework as there can be the feeling that these impact on your sense of ownership and control over your own time.

Knowing what your individual differences and challenges are is the first step in learning how you can improve your time management, focus and organizational skills.

Do you recognize any of the above traits in yourself?

....
....
....
....

Which of these traits affect your time management, focus or organization the most? Or do other issues affect you more? Try to be as specific as possible about what happens for you.

....
....
....
....
....
....
....

FINDING JOY IN STUDYING

What goes well for you in terms of time management, focus or organization?

....
....
....
....
....
....

Are there times you've felt you've focused well or managed your time well? What helped?

....
....
....
....
....
....

What specifically would you like to improve in these areas? Try to be as specific as possible. "Be more organized" is vague. "Organize my lecture notes so I can find what I need quickly" is more specific.

....
....
....
....
....
....

TIME MANAGEMENT, FOCUS AND ORGANIZATION

How would this make things different for you? Be as detailed as you can. What would improve? How would you feel? It's really important you really know why it's important to you so you feel more motivated about meeting your goals.

....
....
....
....
....
....

Now you've investigated what's happening for you and why, it's time to consider what you might like to do to make these issues easier for yourself. Keep in mind your knowledge of your own neurodivergence and consider what might suit you best (or what you could adapt so that the strategy suits you) while you're reading the ideas that follow.

ORGANIZATION

> "I use an app which reminds me of everything I have to do – appointments, studying, chores, eating, taking my meds. It helps me stick to a routine and get everything done."

Let's start by considering organization. It's difficult to manage time well if you don't know when tasks are due or where your resources are. Disorganization can quickly lead to feelings of stress and overwhelm.

Use what's in your pocket

What would have been considered "specialist technology" just a generation back is now likely to be in your pocket. Mobile phones and other digital devices can be a really useful tool when it comes to organizing yourself and managing neurodivergent traits that affect organization and time management.

- **Know you forget to submit assignments on time?** Try to get into the habit of setting yourself alarms or reminders to do so.

- **Walking home and think of the perfect sentences to start your essay?** Send yourself a voice note before you forget it.

- **Do you find it easier to process aural information than written?** Use a screen-reader to listen rather than read.

- **Can you articulate your ideas better orally than when the writing process gets in the way?** Why not try dictating your responses with the speech-to-text function rather than typing? (Though it's often best to proofread before submitting – incorrect transcriptions and punctuation might need to be corrected.)

- **Get easily distracted by notifications or social media?** Try using an app which blocks certain sites or apps for a set amount of time while you work.

Or – ditch the technology

Maybe ditching the technology might prove to be more effective for you! If you find you get so many notifications on your phone that you simply begin to ignore them all, then using reminders and alarms might not be effective for you.

If you know you set an alarm to remind you to study but reach to your phone to silence it and before you know it you've spent an hour replying to messages and scrolling social media, then this might not be the strategy for you. Working onscreen can be distracting for some people, who might find they work better on a printed piece of paper without the digital distractions. Find out what works for you.

Organizing your resources

Studying can be easier if your notes and resources are well organized. You won't waste time trying to find notes from a lecture or looking for a document you know you had the previous week. Some strategies that can support organization include the following:

- Set up digital folders for each class or module.
    - Save all relevant documents in the correct folder so they're easy to find.
- Get into the habit of saving digital documents to a cloud-based system so you can access them on whichever device you're working on.
- Bookmark and save online resources as you find them, so you don't have to waste time searching for them in future.
- Use a folder with dividers for handwritten or printed notes.
    - Label your dividers for each module or subject.
    - File documents in the relevant section as soon as you get them.
    - Alternatively, try using a separate folder for each subject or module.
- Scan / photograph and save paper documents digitally if you think you'll lose the hard copies.
- Have a set place to store physical study notes, textbooks, resources and study equipment.
- Keep your study area as tidy as you can so you can find things easily.
- Take time to explore your school or university's Virtual Learning Environment so you know what resources are available to you.
    - Many universities upload videos of lectures, reading lists and other useful resources for each module.
    - Make yourself aware of the procedures for submitting work and contacting tutors as this can save you time later.

- Find out what software your school or university has installed on their digital devices.
  - Some institutions, for example, have mind mapping software already installed on all machines in their computer suites / libraries.
- Attend any inductions in your college or university's library so you know the resources available and how to access them.

Organizing your calendar

> "I'm an evening person. I know I get more done at that time of day."

Some strategies that can help you feel on top of your workload include the following:

- Choose whether a paper or digital calendar suits you best. The best is whichever you will look at and use regularly.
  - It can help some people to keep everything in one place, rather than having separate "studying" and "free time" diaries, as you can see an overview of everything you have on in a week, which might help you plan more realistically.
- Make a note of deadlines and important dates in your calendar as soon as you are given them so you don't forget to put them in later.
- Schedule slots in your week for independent study so that it gets done.
  - Timetable these as you would for a face-to-face lecture or class you'd be attending.
- Work back from deadlines and note when you need to start tasks.
  - So, if you have an essay due on the 30th of the month and you think it'll take you a week to research, a week to write and then a further week to edit and proofread it, write down those dates too

(e.g. 9th "Research this week", 16th "Write essay this week", 23rd "Edit and proofread this week", 30th "Submit essay").

- That way, you don't get to the due date and realize you've not started a task.

- Set yourself alarms or reminders on your phone if you know you're likely to forget to do tasks or forget to look at your calendar.

- See what works best for you by trying it out and reflecting on what happened.

  - For example, "Was it effective to have separate diaries for my studying and my social life or did it work better to have everything together to give a clearer overview of everything I needed to do in a week?"

- Make it a habit to start a study session by looking at your diary so you can see what's coming up and what you need to prioritize.

Actions

What do you think might be most helpful to you in terms of organization? Are there any ideas from the list above, or do you have other ideas or strategies that have previously been successful for you? Write them down in the tick box table on the following page. You can download this table and use it for different tasks you have actions for.

FINDING JOY IN STUDYING

 MY ACTIONS

Action table:

TIME MANAGEMENT, FOCUS AND ORGANIZATION

Can you get started on any of these actions right now? It can be easy to make lists of things you want to do and then forget about them. Try to get into the habit of actioning things as soon as you can. So, before you move on, what could you do **right now**, while you're thinking about it? Could you grab your phone and set those alarms? Set up some digital folders on your laptop?

> Go do it!

Now tick off any actions you've completed and celebrate these small wins! Tiny steps might not feel like much, but all of these actions together will start to build up and over time will make a bigger difference.

TIME MANAGEMENT

> "I've made my own weekly study plan which helps me organize my week and makes sure I get everything done. I've learned it's important to plan in time for relaxing too."

Effective time management can be key to studying well. If you don't manage your time effectively, some of the following might sound familiar:

- You leave tasks to the last minute and therefore have to rush them, perhaps not completing them to the standard you know you'd be capable of otherwise.

- You feel stressed and overwhelmed by upcoming deadlines.

- You put off tasks and procrastinate.

- You don't prioritize the most important or urgent tasks.

- You spend too much time on tasks that are less important or less relevant.
- You feel disorganized.
- You don't complete tasks in the most efficient way.

Difficulties like these can lead to feelings of stress, anxiety and overwhelm, which can then impact further on your ability to get things done, fuelling a vicious cycle of ineffective time management and stress.

Reading the beginning of this chapter, you might have already identified some of the reasons why you find time management difficult. Many books offer time management strategies such as how to plan out your week and how to prioritize tasks. These can be useful strategies and some are outlined in this chapter, but they don't always work for neurodivergent students – not in isolation anyway – as they don't target the underlying reasons why some neurodivergent individuals encounter difficulties in these areas.

For neurodivergent students, it's often most important to get to know how your neurodivergent brain works and understand how this affects your time management and focus. Once you understand this, you'll find it easier to identify the strategies that might be most useful for you. You'll also – hopefully! – be able to be more self-compassionate to yourself when you encounter difficulties or setbacks – something which can really help improve your wellbeing and lessen negative thoughts about yourself.

Before you start – Is the problem lack of time, or lack of time management?

Before discussing time management, you do first need to check whether the issue is time management – or is it not having enough time to manage in the first place? If you only have two hours in your week to complete independent study, for example, and your course suggests spending 20 hours a week on this, then you're going to have difficulties, even with a whole host of effective time management strategies.

TIME MANAGEMENT, FOCUS AND ORGANIZATION

If you think this is your issue, you could start by filling in the following timetable over the course of a week. Colour code it if that's useful to you. Start by filling in the time you spend:

- sleeping
- working (if you're in paid work)
- in lectures and classes
- commuting
- doing any regular weekly activities you take part in (e.g. religious worship, volunteering, community involvement, hobbies and interests).

Over the next week fill in what you end up doing with the remaining hours.

FINDING JOY IN STUDYING

TIME	MON	TUE	WED
6am - 8am			
8am - 10am			
10am - 12pm			
12pm - 2pm			
2pm - 4pm			
4pm - 6pm			
6pm - 8pm			
8pm - 10pm			
10pm - 6am			

TIME MANAGEMENT, FOCUS AND ORGANIZATION

THU	FRI	SAT	SUN

Now you've a clearer idea of how you spend your week, it might be easier to identify whether you really don't have enough time to devote to studying, or if you do have the time but issues with time management or focus are getting in the way.

If you really don't have the time and your week is completely full of employment, college and other activities, you might have to make some tough decisions.

- Could you reduce the number of hours you work?
- Are there any commitments you could give up for a while?
- Could you take a break from any voluntary work or hobbies until your course finishes?

Of course, decisions like this aren't easy, but if you've made a commitment to studying, it's important you're able to engage fully and make the most of the opportunity. If you need to work in paid employment for more hours than advised by your college or university, speak to your institution's Student Services – they'll be able to advise on any financial support available and can offer guidance specific to your individual situation.

And, if you're having to take a critical look at your weekly schedule, remember to keep some balance. It's important to set aside time for hobbies, socializing and relaxation as these will help your overall wellbeing and stress levels.

Approaching time management

If the issue isn't lack of time, but rather that your neurodivergent traits make it difficult for you to make the most of your time, it's good to start by examining exactly what happens for you when it comes to time management.

 Take some time to explore exactly what happens to you. Try to be as specific as possible. It might be helpful to consider the last few times you've had difficulty with time management. Reflect on these situations below.

TIME MANAGEMENT, FOCUS AND ORGANIZATION

SITUATION 1
What was the task you had to complete?

....

....

How did you plan to approach it?

....

....

What happened instead?

....

....

What was the result?

....

....

SITUATION 2
What was the task you had to complete?

....

....

How did you plan to approach it?

....

....

What happened instead?

....

....

What was the result?

....
....

SITUATION 3
What was the task you had to complete?

....
....

How did you plan to approach it?

....
....

What happened instead?

....
....

What was the result?

....
....

Life happens!
It's important to distinguish between events you can control and those you can't. Circumstances which you have little control over can often impact time management. Illness, accidents, bereavements, family situations, transport delays, ICT failure ... these are all examples of unpredictable events that can affect your plans and take up time you intended to use to study.

First, be kind to yourself in such situations. Getting annoyed at yourself for not being able to study when you've been delayed on public transport for hours will only make you feel worse and won't help the situation. Learn to recognize and accept that these things happen and are out of your control.

If unforeseen circumstances do have a negative impact on your studying, try to let your tutors know as soon as you are able to. Most will be able to offer additional support such as an extended deadline, alternative assignment, or an opportunity to retake an assessment at a later date if needed. However, the sooner you let them know, the better.

Strategies to try

> "I split my day up into three sections and focus on one thing in each time slot. It helps me stop worrying about what's coming up next."

Being aware of your current habits is the first step to making changes.

Next, you can consider what you could do differently to help the situation. Sometimes, simple practical steps such as setting a regular alarm, or attending a useful workshop, might be enough.

For other situations you might decide to work on introducing a new strategy or changing a habit, a thinking pattern or your mindset around something. Often, you'll need to try out a few different strategies before you find out what suits you. You might need to combine different ideas or adapt them so they work better for you. Some examples of possible useful strategies are included on the following pages.

- Remember, not every strategy will be useful for every individual, and you won't need to try everything. Read through and decide on which you think might be most useful to you, or use these ideas as starting points to come up with your own ideas.

If you don't understand what to do

If you don't understand what you have to do for a task, or haven't understood the topic you've got to write an assignment on, it's likely to affect your time management. Perhaps you won't want to get started because you feel you won't be able to do it. Maybe you'll spend a lot of time worrying about it and not wanting to ask for help. Or perhaps you'll make a start but just can't complete the task as you don't understand the content. If you haven't understood, it's important to ask for help sooner rather than later.

You could:

- ask a course tutor for support. Some might have specific weekly "office hours" when they're available for questions
- speak to your SENCo or Disability Officer for ideas of what could help you understand when in class or lectures
- attend catch-up or revision sessions
- attend workshops on specific study skills such as note-taking or research skills
- watch any lectures or read notes from anything you've missed due to absence
- ask a peer on your course to explain something
- re-read your notes and seek out books, articles, videos or resources that explain the topic in a different way.

If you underestimate

Perhaps you tend to drastically underestimate the time a task will take. You set aside an hour to write an essay and find you only manage to plan it out in that time. You go to the library for half an hour before a lecture starts, only to find you've barely logged in to the catalogue search before it's time to go. If you often underestimate how long a task will take, the starting point is to become aware of this. Perhaps you put aside an hour to write an essay, then realize that you only get it planned out in that time. Start to note how long various academic tasks actually do take you. There is an activity you can complete to help with this on the next page.

TIME MANAGEMENT, FOCUS AND ORGANIZATION

Once you've identified underestimating as a problem, you can begin to notice your thoughts and actions and replace them with a more realistic timeframe.

- Do you notice yourself thinking "I'll write up the report in the half hour before the class it's due in"?

- Catch these sorts of thoughts and remind yourself: "Ah, I often underestimate how long these things will take. I have an hour this evening to start on it and then I'll go to the library for another hour before class tomorrow too."

- Once you realize you underestimate, get into the habit of scheduling longer periods of time in your calendar for each task.

Time management table:

Task	How long I usually set aside for this task	A more realistic amount of time required for this task
Example: Finding relevant journal articles in the library	*Example:* 15 minutes on the way to a lecture	*Example:* Up to an hour of designated time

TIME MANAGEMENT, FOCUS AND ORGANIZATION

If you're easily side-tracked

- Did you go home intending to study but sat down on the sofa and, before you knew it, two hours had passed watching television?
- Did you go to the library but bumped into a friend and went for a coffee instead?

You might have the best of intentions to study but other – more interesting – things always seem to come up. If you know you intend to study but then sit down and get engrossed in binge-watching Netflix or chatting to those around you, consider what could help break this pattern.

Telling yourself you won't engage next time is unlikely to be enough. You might need to change a habit or routine so you're less likely to encounter the distraction. Maybe you could start going directly to the library after lectures instead of going home to study, so that these distractions don't occur? Consider what could work best for your individual circumstances.

If you get "stuck" or encounter problems

If you're someone who starts well but comes to a standstill when you encounter problems, consider who you could ask for help and how you can ask them.

- Peers on your course might be able to clarify what was discussed in class.
- Course tutors could answer queries related to the work set.
- Assignment guidelines, assessment criteria and lists of useful reading and resources might be available to download from your Virtual Learning Environment (VLE) for each module.
- The university's library service can answer questions you have about locating resources or using library services, or might even have online videos or blogs on their website or VLE explaining how to do this.

Filling in the table on the next page will help you to identify sources of support and how to contact them.

Things that I get "stuck" on:	Who could help with this:	How or when I can contact them:

If you get overwhelmed by a large task
If a task seems too big, it can be difficult to know where to start. A task such as "Prepare a presentation" might seem overwhelming. It might help if you break down larger tasks into smaller steps. "Prepare a presentation" can sound like a task that's going to take ages, but if you break it down into smaller steps it can feel more manageable. For example:

1. Choose a topic from the list.
2. Read my notes and the textbook page on this topic.
3. Decide on five sections to talk about and so on…

These are all smaller tasks that can be more easily started and ticked off your list.

Breaking larger tasks up into smaller steps is a good habit to get into. Writing these smaller tasks in your diary or calendar rather than the big task might help you get started and stay focused as you work through each step.

TIME MANAGEMENT, FOCUS AND ORGANIZATION

Task separation table:

My bigger task is:

Smaller steps to complete this	Resources or equipment I'll need	Date to do this
1.		
2.		
3.		
4.		
5.		
6.		
7.		

If you have too much to do!
If you look at your to-do list and feel there is just too much to do, consider what could help with this. Here are some things you could try.

- Be realistic about how much is achievable in one day. Putting ten tasks on your to-do list when you only have time to complete three will leave you feeling overwhelmed and behind.
- You might find a smaller list for each day seems more manageable than a long list of everything they need to do for the week or term.
- You may like to split your day into "slots" and do one specific task in each slot of time, so that you're creating their own timetable:
  - e.g. 9–10 read lecture notes, 10–12 attend lecture, 12–1 lunch, 1–3 prepare presentation
- Keeping all your lists and deadlines in one diary or calendar might be helpful to reduce overwhelm rather than having multiple lists for different things.
- Prioritizing can be really useful. Remove from your list any tasks that are unnecessary or unimportant. We'll look at prioritizing more later in this chapter.
- Make a "could-do" list of less important tasks which can feel like less pressure than a "to-do" list.
- You could start with the quick and easy tasks on your list that can be ticked off relatively easily so you have the feeling of moving through your to-dos quickly.
- Or maybe you would prefer to get a bigger – or more anxiety-provoking – task out the way first so that it is a load off your mind. What would help you feel less overwhelmed?
- If there are tasks that you consistently put to the bottom of your to-do list, think about why this is happening.
  - Does this task actually need to be done – can it be removed?
  - Are you stuck on something – where could you get support?
  - What else could you do to stop this task becoming overwhelming?

TIME MANAGEMENT, FOCUS AND ORGANIZATION

If you're a perfectionist

So, first of all, wanting to do things to the best of your ability is certainly not a negative! It's great that you want to produce the best work you can and it is a real positive.

However, perfectionist traits can sometimes go so far that they actually prevent you completing a task. For example, you might find you spend so long trying to make your first paragraph "perfect" that you don't actually get the essay finished. Or you might worry so much about your work not being "perfect" that you keep starting and re-starting the piece. Maybe you decide that you won't get 100 per cent so there's no point even handing the piece in.

If you find your perfectionist traits can verge on being unhelpful, there are various things you could try that might help. For example, you could:

- **speak to a mentor, coach or counsellor** about how your perfectionist traits impact you and work on strategies to move forwards

- **become aware of any unhelpful thoughts or actions** that relate to having high standards for yourself

- **challenge any unhelpful beliefs** around needing to be "perfect":
  - "Okay, so this is a formative essay, so it's not supposed to be perfect – the whole point is to get useful feedback from my tutor before the final version"
  - "I'm worried this isn't good enough but I know I've worked hard on it. And actually I always worry but end up getting good marks"
  - "Right, I was upset that I didn't get full marks, but if I could already do all this stuff perfectly, there'd be no point me being a student"

- **ensure your goals are realistic:**
  - if you're setting goals around the grades you're aiming for or the amount of time you're going to study, be honest with yourself whether these are realistic or not

- **set yourself a time limit** if you tend to spend too long going over and over work:
  - "Okay, I'm going to spend an hour proofreading and improving this essay and then I will stop as it's important for me to start the next piece of work, have a rest or spend time on my hobbies"
  - tell yourself, "I know I have already put the time and effort into this piece and it is good enough to hand in"
- **learn to prioritize** the most important aspects of a task and change your self-talk around these:
  - "Okay, I want to show my knowledge about this topic, but this question is only worth three marks, so I just need to make the main points and then move on"
  - "I'd love to make a well-designed slideshow to supplement my presentation, but I'm getting marked on content, not design. If I don't have time to add in amazing visuals, it really won't make a difference to my grades."

Processing time

It's also helpful to be aware whether the amount of time you are allocating for different tasks is realistic *for you*. Some neurodivergent individuals need more processing time than neurotypical individuals to understand either spoken and / or written language.

Some, for example, find it hard to make sense of spoken information, even if they understand the individual words used. Others might have a similar problem when reading – they've understood the words but find they need longer to process what it all actually means.

This can lead to difficulties such as not being able to respond to immediate "on the spot" questions, or not feeling able to keep up in group discussions and seminars. You might need to allocate additional time for some tasks, or research possible software which could support you.

See Chapter 5 for ideas of how to manage reading and note-taking tasks. Letting your tutors know of your difficulties can also make a difference and might help to take some of the pressure off in class.

Prioritizing

Being able to prioritize tasks effectively is one aspect of time management. Prioritizing means doing the urgent and important tasks first. Often these will be the ones with the closest deadline. Prioritizing is also about ensuring the most important steps of a task are completed before the least important.

For example, if you're making a poster in class, it's usually more important to add the information first, rather than starting with designing an intricate border and not getting around to adding any actual content.

Using a diary or calendar effectively can help you identify which tasks you need to prioritize, as you'll be able to see upcoming deadlines and activities all in one place.

PRIORITIZING DEADLINES

In the following table, consider all the homework tasks, assignments or projects you currently have to complete. Then write the date they are due. Consider the importance and urgency of each one, then number them in the order you'll have to prioritize them.

You can download and re-use this table to decide the order of tasks within a project. Some tasks will have to be done in a certain order (for example, you can't proofread a piece of work that hasn't been written yet) and some tasks might need to take priority over others (for example, if you're working to a tight deadline, you might need to concentrate on getting the key information into your assignment rather than spending time on the design or on additional research around a very minor point).

Task prioritization table:

Tasks	Date due by	Order of priority

FOCUS

> "I like the same routine each week. It helps me focus and keeps me on top of my workload."

So, we've looked at strategies for organization and for time management. Let's turn now to focus. Concentration and focus can be difficult for many neurodivergent students. You might be somebody who has difficulty staying focused on one task, you might be somebody who hyperfocuses, or you might experience both at different times, depending on what it is you're working on and on other factors.

Improving focus and concentration

First, analyse exactly what happens for you. Think to a recent time when you've had difficulty staying focused on a task. When was it?

....
....
....

What is it that happened? Were you distracted by social media notifications? Did you get distracted by other people? Or were the distractions more internal – you started to feel bored, you thought something else was more exciting to start, you daydreamed or started worrying or thinking about something else? Do you feel like you have no control over focusing, as some people describe with autistic inertia? Note down what happened for you:

....
....
....
....

Now consider what might be helpful. Some neurodivergent students find some of the following ideas helpful. It's worth repeating that not everything will be relevant for every individual. Consider your individual needs and circumstances.

Remove or reduce external distractions

It's an obvious place to start but shouldn't be forgotten – you could try removing or reducing some of the things that distract you.

- If you're easily distracted by others, could you try working in a quiet space such as a quiet study area or a library?
- If others who you live with distract you, try asking them not to disturb you for a set amount of time.
- If you're easily distracted by music or television, could you turn these off for the duration of your study session?
- Could you try working in a tidy, clutter-free area so you're not distracted by the things around you?
- Could you keep your phone or other digital devices in a different room while you're studying or set them to silent?
- Could you log out of apps and social media for the time you're studying?
- Could you use apps or software which allow you to disable certain websites or apps for a duration so that you're not tempted to check in?

Reduce as many "internal distractions" as possible

Wandering thoughts

If you find your thoughts wandering, especially if you're worrying about something, could you set aside "worry time" for later in the day?

Tell yourself, "Okay, I recognize I'm worrying about (that problem) again. I'm studying now, so I'll worry about that later, at 6pm."

Some people find that once their "worry time" comes around, they actually don't feel as worried about whatever it was after all!

TIME MANAGEMENT, FOCUS AND ORGANIZATION

Empty your head
Start a study session by "emptying your head". Before you sit down to study, write down a list of anything else you need to do or think about later that day, so you're not trying to hold other things in your head while you're studying.

Thoughts
If thoughts keep popping into your head about things to do, for example "I must reply to that message" or "I must book that appointment" etc, and you interrupt your studies to action the thought, try to get into the habit of making a note of whatever it is you need to do rather than breaking off and doing it. Then re-focusing on your studying. After your study session, go through your list and follow up anything you need to then.

If you have a bigger worry or anxiety that takes over your thoughts, seek support from a counsellor, coach or mentor to discuss this.

Improve your focus

> "Using the pomodoro technique works for me."

The pomodoro technique
This technique was developed by Francesco Cirillo in the late 1980s to aid focus. It breaks down work into 25-minute intervals, each followed by a short break.

1. Set a timer for 25 minutes and try to stay focused on the task in hand for this period of time.

   Tip! If you find yourself distracted (you probably will!), simply notice this ("Oh! I've come to the window to see what that noise is but I'm in the middle of a pomodoro – back to it!" or "I've reached for my phone to check TikTok but I'm doing a pomodoro – I'll wait until this 25 minutes is up") and then refocus on your task.

2. After the 25 minutes, take a five minute break.

3. Repeat this sequence three or four times before taking a longer break for 15 to 30 minutes.

Some students find this technique helps them to stay focused. Different lengths of time might suit you better.

> **Tip!** Avoid using timers if you know these will feel like too much pressure to you or if you think you'll be clock-watching rather than focusing on your task.

Study at the time of day that you know your focus is best
For some this might be morning, for others in the afternoon or evening. Working with your natural inclinations can help with focus and energy levels.

> **Tip!** Do you know you lack energy after socializing or a day at college? Schedule in rest time.
> Do you know you feel energized after exercise or being with people? Use that energy to get things done.

Set a clear target for your study session in advance
If you recognize that it takes you a long time to decide what to work on, set your goal in advance (e.g. "In tomorrow's study session I am going to plan my geography essay").

> **Tip!** Write this in your diary or planner so you know what you're going to do and don't waste time trying to decide.

"What one thing"
If you're really struggling to get started and don't feel like studying, consider "what one thing" you could do to move forward. It might be as simple as typing up the title to your essay and a few sub-headings, or reserving a book you need from the library. Some students find that making a start then builds momentum and they end up carrying on and getting more done than they imagined. Even if you don't, you've at least done something that will move you towards your goal. Small steps all add up.

Be accountable

Some students find their concentration improves if they are "accountable" to somebody else. Perhaps you work better if you attend a homework club or study in a library or know that somebody is going to check on you?

> "Body doubling has been a game-changer for me."

Tip! Try body doubling. It is a technique many people find useful – working alongside somebody else (on different tasks) can help them stay focused.

Mix it up

If you feel you need novelty, you might find mixing up strategies or changing where you study or who with can make it easier to feel focused.

Gamification

Do you respond well to games or challenges? How could you turn your studying tasks into more of a game? For example:

- Creating a "reward chart" for you to "move up to the next level" each time you complete a task?

- Racing against the clock? Challenge yourself to stay completely focused for ten minutes. Could you increase this by a minute the next time? And then another minute? See if you can beat your previous best each time.

- Finding friends who you can "compete" with? (For example, who can stay focused for the longest before checking their phone? The "winner" gets to choose what's for dinner.)

Sensory sensitivities

If you're distracted by sensory sensitivities, can you organize your study area to reduce this discomfort? Where can you work that suits you best?

Medication

You might be offered medication to treat some ADHD symptoms. Some people find this really does help them stay focused, others find it doesn't help or that the side-effects outweigh any benefits. Some people find the effects are greatest when used in combination with other strategies and support.

If you are offered medication, it's important to discuss this thoroughly with your GP or healthcare professional. Consider what sort of questions you will want to ask:

- What could the benefits be?
- How long will it take to notice any benefits?
- What are common side-effects?
- Will it interact with other medications?
- What symptoms will the medication help, and which will it not?
- What different options are available?

How to work with hyperfocus

See the positives!

Hyperfocus can be a real strength if it's related to a subject you're studying. If you're really interested in a topic and doing lots of extra reading and research, that's great! Just try to learn to be aware if it does have any negative impact on anything else (for example, it means you go to bed too late or don't get work for other subjects done) and do what you can to limit the impact of this.

Set a timer

If you tend to hyperfocus on studying and find that you then forget to do other things that need to be done or have difficulty shifting your attention, try setting an alarm, timer or reminder when you'd like to stop to prompt you to move on to another task.

Do the quicker or more boring tasks first

If you know you're likely to hyperfocus on a certain topic or activity, try getting any other smaller but important tasks done first, so that it matters less if you end up spending longer on the task that interests you.

Assess what you spent your time on at the end of a study session

Some students find they spend a lot of time focusing on one small detail, which will only be a small percentage of their final marks, leaving themselves no time to get the biggest part of an assignment done.

If this happens to you, consider what might help. Could you split your next study session into smaller time slots and give yourself a specific task for each slot so you ensure you get everything done?

Hyperfocus – but not on studying

If you tend to hyperfocus on things that aren't related to your studying, some of the above ideas might be useful as well. You could:

- try getting your studying done first to allow yourself uninterrupted time on your other focus

- or set yourself a timer when it's time to move on to your studying (if you're likely to respond to this).

You could also see what you could do to make studying more attractive – would you be more likely to get it done with friends, or in a library? And even if you hyperfocus on something completely unrelated to your studying, it might still be possible to use this to help you with your studies.

Perhaps you could link your special interest to your area of study? Or maybe you could use it to practise study-related skills such as research, reading, planning and written or spoken communication?

Digital tools

Many apps exist which are designed to support organization, focus and time management, and new ones continue to be launched all the time. It can be difficult to know where to begin and which to try out. Some schools, colleges and universities have subscriptions to useful apps and software, so it might be useful to speak to your college's librarian, student support officers or disability officer to find out what's available to you and what might be most helpful for your specific needs. Some students might receive funding through their Disability Support Allowance for specialist apps or software.

Before deciding what to use, particularly if there is a cost to yourself involved, decide what will work for you best. Ask yourself questions such as:

- What specifically do I need support with?
- Do I need all the additional features? Will these be useful or will they be a distraction?
- Do I feel overwhelmed with notifications?
- Will this feel like one more thing to do / an additional task?
- Can I access this across devices / outside the university?
- Will I actually remember to use this?

Digital technologies are great – life-changing for many students – but only if they actually make things easier for you. If you've been recommended something that you don't feel saves you time, then you don't have to use it. Ask about other options or strategies.

ACTION PLANNING

Now it's time to decide which strategies might be useful to you. Read through the strategies in this chapter again and consider any other techniques that you've tried in the past or heard about from others. There might be some you'd like to adapt so they better suit you. Try not to be disheartened if you don't find the right technique straight away. New habits take a while to get used to. Some things might be more effective for certain tasks or at different times. Other things you might need to adapt as you go along. Try to see it as a continuous cycle of identifying what's not working, trying out new strategies, continuing with those that work and refining those that don't work so well.

THINK
What's the current situation?
What needs to change?

PLAN
What are you going to try?

DO
Try it out!

REVIEW
What worked? (What things can you repeat next time?)
What didn't work?

Verdict table part 1:

What I will try first is:

(Once you've tried this strategy, reflect below)

What worked for me was:
-
-
-
-
-

What didn't work well was:
-
-
-
-
-

VERDICT

These methods/structures worked really well for me! I'll try these again. ☐

There were some positives. Next time I'll utilize what worked well and adjust what didn't. ☐

These methods/structures probably aren't right for me at this point in time. ☐

TIME MANAGEMENT, FOCUS AND ORGANIZATION

 Verdict table part 2:

What I will try first is:

(Once you've tried this strategy, reflect below)

What worked for me was:
-
-
-
-
-

What didn't work well was:
-
-
-
-
-

VERDICT

These methods/structures worked really well for me! I'll try these again. ☐

There were some positives. Next time I'll utilize what worked well and adjust what didn't. ☐

These methods/structures probably aren't right for me at this point in time. ☐

Verdict table part 3:

What I will try first is:

(Once you've tried this strategy, reflect below)

What worked for me was:
-
-
-
-
-

What didn't work well was:
-
-
-
-
-

VERDICT

These methods/structures worked really well for me! I'll try these again. ☐

There were some positives. Next time I'll utilize what worked well and adjust what didn't. ☐

These methods/structures probably aren't right for me at this point in time. ☐

TIME MANAGEMENT, FOCUS AND ORGANIZATION

SUMMARY

In this chapter, you've learned:

- Time management, prioritizing, organization and focus are closely linked.

- These issues can be problematic for many students, but especially those who are neurodivergent.

- Difficulties might arise from traits such as: hyperfocus, difficulties focusing, time blindness, difficulties shifting attention, executive functioning difficulties, perfectionism, overthinking and procrastination.

- Being aware of your own tendencies is the first step in making changes.

- You often won't find the perfect strategy straight away. You might need to try out several different things and adapt them to see what works for you.

- If you're experiencing anxiety or stress and this is affecting your wellbeing, be sure to seek specialist support to work on any underlying issues.

What are the key things you've learned about yourself from this chapter in relation to time management, organization or focus?

....
....
....
....
....

What are the top three strategies you're going to take forwards?

....

....

....

....

....

Chapter 5

READING AND NOTE-TAKING

This chapter takes a deep dive into the realms of reading and note-taking. These skills become more important when you study at higher levels as more independent study is required.

A SUPER-QUICK OVERVIEW

Note-taking
Note-taking might be required in various situations. For example, you might need to take notes in class or at lectures so you have a record of what was taught. You might also need to make notes when you are reading a text or watching a video independently. These notes will then be used when you revise for an exam, prepare for a seminar or write up an assignment. Writing effective notes involves being able to identify the key points from the information given and note this information down in a quick way that makes sense to you and that you can use for the purpose required.

Reading
Reading around your subject is necessary to gain the in-depth knowledge needed for assignments and examinations at higher levels. Reading involves different skills and techniques. For example, you might need to:

- identify which are the most relevant texts or parts of the text

- skim and scan a text to get the gist
- pull out specific facts or information
- identify an author's arguments or biases
- analyse the purpose and reliability of a text.

Research

Research can take many different forms, depending on your subject and level of study. You might have to research a topic through reading books and journals, watching relevant videos, searching on the web or listening to podcasts. You'll need to be able to locate the resources most relevant to you and assess the suitability and reliability of each source, before identifying and analysing the useful information.

Research can also mean your own investigations. You might have to create your own research questions and gather information to answer these. This might be through using questionnaires / surveys, conducting interviews, carrying out observations, analysing data or conducting experiments. There'll be specific safety, practical and ethical guidelines to follow and you'll have to ensure any investigations are valid and reliable.

We'll now take a closer look at reading and note-taking and investigate common difficulties and issues that arise.

READING

> "I understand the words but can't seem to process the overall meaning."

You'll likely have to do quite a bit of reading when studying at higher levels. Depending on your subject this might include:

- textbooks / academic books

READING AND NOTE-TAKING

- books related to your subject
- academic journal articles
- newspaper reports
- webpages
- magazine articles
- business reports
- research papers and reports
- documents containing advice, guidance or regulations from the government or other organizations
- primary sources: archives, letters, diaries, interview transcriptions and other documents.

Becoming aware of your reading

> "I never seem to be able to remember what I read."

1. Choose a short text to read.

   It doesn't have to be anything related to your studying – a general news article will work well for this activity. Choose a non-fiction text on a topic that's unfamiliar to you, rather than a piece of fiction or something you already know a lot about.

2. Read the article or chapter in your usual way and then think about:

   a. How did you read this article? (Did you read quickly or slowly? Did you focus on every word and sentence, or just get the general gist? Did you skip parts?)

   ....

   ....

....
....
....

b. What did you do if you encountered any new vocabulary or concepts? (Did you try to work out the meaning from the context? Did you look up a definition? Did you just gloss over it without understanding?)

....
....
....
....
....

c. What were you thinking or feeling about the content as you read? (Did you agree or disagree with what the author was saying? Were you outraged by the topic or argument? Did you find the topic evoked strong feelings?)

....
....
....
....
....

What did you notice from this activity? It's all about becoming aware of how you tend to read. If you notice you tend to skip over unfamiliar vocabulary, this might not matter so much when you're reading a general news article or book, but it might be something you'll need to do differently if you're reading an article in detail to prepare for a seminar. If you have strong feelings when you're reading about a topic, you might need to become aware of these feelings and consider if they mean you're possibly reading with bias or preconceived ideas. Why do you feel the way you do? Are your feelings or beliefs about a topic meaning that you're less willing to take on board opposing arguments, or that you're paying more attention to information that supports your perspective? This might be important when you come to write up assignments that need to take a balanced view.

Reading for studying

You're probably already seeing how reading for studying is different from general reading. When you're studying, you're usually reading with a more specific purpose. For example:

- to pick out specific facts or statistics
- to gain background context of an issue
- to pick out different arguments, debates and perspectives
- to evaluate evidence or research
- to find out what has already been written about a topic and identify any gaps
- to compare policy, research and practice.

Asking yourself **why** you're reading something can help you choose the most appropriate strategy and ensures you're reading more purposefully.

Approaching reading

> "Academic articles look so boring, long and dense. Puts me off before I've even begun."

Before you begin to read, you need to decide **how** you're going to read. There are different kinds of reading and some are more suited to a particular purpose than others. Reading in the most appropriate way can save a lot of time. Three approaches to reading discussed here are scanning, skimming and focused reading.

Scanning

When you **scan** a text, you're not looking at every word. You're scanning it to get the overall gist of what it's about and the arguments the piece puts forward. You might look at sub-headings, chapter headings or read the first sentence of each paragraph to get an idea of the debates. Scanning a text in this way can be useful to decide whether or not it's worth reading it in more detail. Starting by reading in detail might mean you waste time on reading a piece that actually turns out to be irrelevant to your needs.

Skimming

If you're **skimming** a text, you're looking for a specific section or topic. You might skim for key words relating to a particular question you have to answer, or might skim the text to find some information you remember you've previously read. Skimming can be useful if you are looking for something specific in a text.

Focused reading

Focused reading, in comparison, is slower. You read while thinking about and reflecting on the information. This type of reading takes longer than scanning or skimming. You might be making notes at the same time or thinking about how it relates to what you've already learned or to an assignment question you need to answer. You're reading to understand.

So, the first thing to decide is how you're going to read a text. Next, you'll need to use appropriate strategies to ensure you understand, process and retain the information in a suitable way.

Reading strategies

"I get bored reading!"

Reading for academic purposes involves understanding what you're reading, so you can explain, analyse and evaluate it in your own work. Some common issues students can experience when reading are:

- maintaining focus and concentration

READING AND NOTE-TAKING

- difficulty identifying the key points
- not understanding unfamiliar vocabulary or concepts
- feeling overwhelmed by the amount to read
- not being able to make sense of the information
- not recalling or remembering what has been read
- difficulties with decoding words and reading speed (often associated with dyslexia).

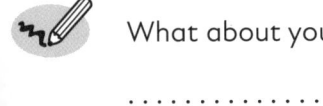

What about you? Do you regularly experience any difficulties?

....
....
....
....
....

Have you used any strategies in the past that have helped? Has there been anything previous teachers have suggested that has worked for you?

....
....
....
....
....

Possible useful strategies

> "I listen to texts (using a screen-reader) rather than read on screen. I find it much quicker and I understand more."

Decoding and reading speed

If you're dyslexic, a specialist dyslexia advisor in your college or university should be able to help you develop suitable strategies to support with reading. Some students (especially those who are dyslexic, but others too) find it easier to listen rather than read, so you could try using the text-to-speech or the screen-reader function on your device to listen to information if this is quicker for you.

Some students also find that the font, background colour, size of text or a coloured overlay can make a difference, so experiment with this if you think it could help you.

If speed is an issue, get into the habit of setting aside more time to complete reading tasks. Check with your SENCo or Disability Advisor to assess whether you're eligible for extra time in assessments and examinations.

Slow down

If you've noticed you've a habit of reading quickly, consider whether this affects your understanding. It can be tempting to rush through reading to get it done, but sometimes just slowing down, really thinking about each paragraph and avoiding distractions can be enough to improve your understanding. Check back to the section on "focus" in the previous chapter for some ideas.

Vocabulary

Unfamiliar vocabulary can be a barrier to understanding what you're reading. Academic texts in particular can be full of subject-specific terminology which you might not yet be familiar with. The suggestions below might help.

- Look at the context.
  - Can you work out meaning from the rest of the sentence / paragraph?
- Look at the word.
  - Can you work out the meaning from identifying the root word, prefix or suffix? (E.g. you might know the meaning of "decisive", so

work out that "indecisive" means the opposite, or if you know the meaning of "employ" you might then be able to work out meanings of words such as "employee", "employer" and "unemployment".)

- Use a dictionary (either paper or online) which will give you a definition of a word.
    - Sometimes words can have specific meanings when used in academia, so be aware that a general dictionary might not tell you exactly what the word means in your specific context.

- Look at the glossary.
    - Textbooks often include a glossary (often at the back of the book or end of each chapter) which gives meanings of subject-specific vocabulary used throughout the text.

- Find a subject-specific resource, vocabulary list or website.
    - Useful resources might be listed on course materials given to you by tutors.
    - If you're finding resources yourself, check that they have been produced by a reliable organization or suitably qualified individual. Plenty of inaccurate information exists, especially on the internet.

Sentence structure

Written text, especially academic texts, often use far more complicated sentence structure than is used in everyday communication. This can make some texts much more difficult to process and understand.

- First check whether there are any unfamiliar vocabulary items in the sentence that are impeding your understanding.

- Re-read the sentence several times slowly. Reading a sentence out loud can sometimes be helpful.

- Split the sentence up into shorter parts and work on understanding each part.

Here's an example of a complex academic sentence:

> Despite the potential of artificial intelligence to revolutionize various industries by automating tasks and optimizing processes, ethical concerns surrounding its development and deployment, such as algorithmic bias and potential job displacement, necessitate careful consideration and proactive implementation of frameworks that ensure responsible and equitable implementation of these technologies.

Your first step might be to identify any vocabulary that's new to you (e.g. "algorithmic bias" or "equitable") to see if that helps you make sense of the sentence. Then you might need to split the sentence up into the different clauses (often split up by commas) and consider each one separately. For example:

> Despite the potential of artificial intelligence to revolutionize various industries by automating tasks and optimizing processes...

So, this is saying that artificial intelligence has the potential to revolutionize various industries. It will do this by automating tasks and optimizing processes.

> ...ethical concerns surrounding its development and deployment, such as algorithmic bias and potential job displacement...

And in this part of the sentence the "such as" is referring to the ethical concerns. So examples of ethical concerns are algorithmic bias and potential job displacement.

> ...necessitate careful consideration and proactive implementation of frameworks...

This part is saying that the ethical concerns mean that frameworks will have to be considered and put into place.

> ...that ensure responsible and equitable implementation of these technologies.
>
> And these frameworks must ensure that the artificial intelligence technologies are used responsibly and equitably.
>
> So, overall, the sentence is basically explaining how artificial intelligence has the potential to improve things, but there are ethical concerns about its use. This means that people will have to consider carefully how to implement these technologies in a fair and responsible way. Breaking a longer sentence down like this into its subclauses and thinking about each one separately can be a helpful way of understanding.

Too much to read

If you're overwhelmed by lots of information, consider what could work for you.

First check you're only reading what you need to and are using the most appropriate reading strategy. You won't always need to read every word. If scanning or skimming the text would be more appropriate at this point, employ one of those strategies.

Use sub-headings to locate the most relevant sections. Journal articles contain an abstract – this gives a summary of the article and might be all you need to read to decide whether or not it is a useful and relevant enough article for you to read the rest of the article in detail.

- Set aside sufficient time for reading tasks so you don't feel rushed.

- Break down reading tasks into smaller chunks. Maybe reading one chapter or shorter section at a time and then taking a break or completing a different task would work for you?

- Could you try covering part of the text up with a piece of paper (or changing the font size on screen) so you focus on one paragraph at a time?

- Read with a purpose in mind. Are you reading to answer specific questions? Are you looking for certain information? Knowing what you're looking for and why you are reading might make the process feel less overwhelming.

- Worrying about a task can often be more stressful than actually doing it! Sometimes once you get started, things can seem less overwhelming.

Recalling and remembering

A common difficulty can be reading a text but then not being able to recall or remember what you've read. So, what can help with this?

Try to read without distractions

It's much harder to remember something if you weren't totally engaged with it. Research has shown that multi-tasking or constantly switching between tasks (even if the "tasks" only take a few seconds, like checking a social media app) when studying and reading negatively affects your attention, working memory, reading comprehension and recall (May and Elder, 2018). So, try to get into the habit of reading without distractions to give yourself the best possible chance of remembering what you're reading.

Don't forget the basics

You're less likely to remember things accurately when you're tired or feeling stressed, so try to schedule reading tasks for when you're feeling more energized.

It's hard to remember what you don't understand

Look up definitions for unfamiliar vocabulary and break down longer sentences into short chunks.

Get an overview

It might be easier to read something if you have a general overview first – reading a chapter summary or the abstract first might be helpful, or flicking through sub-headings to give you an idea of what's coming up and everything that is covered.

Try reading a printed version
Evidence suggests that some people remember more and understand more of what they've read in a printed book rather than what they've read onscreen (Clinton, 2019), particularly when reading non-fiction, so try and see if this helps you.

Pause to think
After reading each section, get into the habit of pausing and thinking about what you've just read. Can you put it into your own words (either in your head, out loud or in notes)? If you can, you've likely understood it. If you can't, go back and work on understanding before moving on and reading a whole text that you're struggling with.

Try out various strategies and see what helps you remember

- Does it help to highlight key words or phrases?
- Perhaps you like to annotate a text with your notes as you go along?
- If you find visuals help you, could you try to summarize what you're reading in a mind-map, flow chart or diagram?
- Perhaps you like to summarize what you've read at the end of each chapter or section?

Engaging with the reading material in your own way will help you understand what you're reading and remember more.

Focus and concentration
You might like to look back at the previous chapter if you feel you'd benefit from improving your focus and concentration when reading.

Once you've identified your particular challenges when reading, consider what could help. Could you get into the habit of looking up unfamiliar words? Does it help to make notes or diagrams when you read? What about highlighting or annotations? Do you prefer to use a screen-reader and listen rather than read? A printed copy or read onscreen? Do you find the pomodoro technique helpful? You might find the chapter on "Time management, focus and organization" or the upcoming section on "Note-taking" helpful too.

 Which strategies would you like to try next time you read for academic purposes?

Reading critically

When you read for academic purposes, you're not only reading to understand the text. Especially when studying at higher levels, you'll also have to evaluate what you're reading. For example, at a basic level, it's important to be able to distinguish between fact and opinion when you're reading.

Questions to ask
When you're reading for academic purposes, what questions do you think you need to ask yourself about the text?

Reading critically means asking **why** a text was written and evaluating its reliability. You might ask yourself questions such as:

- **Who wrote this?** Are they an expert on the subject? Who do they work for?

- **Why was this written?** Who funded the research? Is it promoting an organization or product?

- **Where was this published?** In a reputable academic journal? A personal blog? In local media etc?

- **When was this written?** Is the information still up-to-date?

- **What is the purpose of this text?** Was it written to inform, persuade or entertain?

- **Is there bias?** Does the author promote a personal, political or organizational opinion? Are different perspectives considered?

- **How was any research undertaken?** What were the research methods? How many people were surveyed? How was the sample chosen? Is it valid and reliable?

- **Are claims backed up?** Is there clear evidence for claims, i.e. references or research studies?

- **Are experts who are quoted named?** Who are they and do they have a vested interest?

Try it out. Find an article related to your studies. Read it. Can you answer any of the following questions about the article?

Who wrote this?

....

....

When was this written?

....

....

Where was this published?

....

....

Why was this published?

....

....

What is the purpose of this article?

....

....

Is there bias?

....

....

How was the research undertaken?

....

....

Are the claims backed up?

....

....

Who are the experts referred to?

....

....

Other thoughts?

....

....

READING AND NOTE-TAKING

Getting into the habit of reading with these sort of questions in mind can help you engage more critically with the text. Reading critically also involves reading with an awareness of your own opinions, as well as being able to recognize the author's opinions.

Your own opinions about a topic can influence how you read. For example, you might be more likely to accept and include ideas and research that you agree with, and reject research that doesn't fit with your personal opinions.

Consider your personal opinions related to the subjects or topics you're studying. For example, imagine you're studying a module on environmental sustainability. You might feel strongly that individuals need to take greater responsibility for decreasing their consumption and recycling more, or you might believe that larger organizations need to take greater responsibility for producing longer-lasting goods with less packaging.

Once you've identified your beliefs, consider what has influenced these. Strong beliefs can come from personal past experiences, your peer group, family members, the community, educational experiences, or the media, including social media. If you notice your beliefs come from a particular media source, it can be worth questioning the reliability and bias of this source. Are you getting a balanced view? Social media algorithms in particular can keep feeding us "more of the same" rather than providing users with different perspectives.

You can consider and reflect on this using the table on the next page and download it to re-use if you'd like to.

FINDING JOY IN STUDYING

 Strong beliefs table:

Topic:

Beliefs/opinions I hold:	Where these originate:

READING AND NOTE-TAKING

It's certainly not wrong to have personal beliefs and it might even be your strong convictions that have motivated you to study a subject. Being aware of your personal opinions just helps to ensure that you keep an open mind and are able to weigh up the evidence fairly and in an unbiased manner. This is an important part of higher-level research and study and can ensure your arguments are robust.

NOTE-TAKING

> "I try to make notes but can't keep up."

How do you currently take notes? (e.g. by hand or on a digital device, highlighting, noting key words, using diagrams, using abbreviations…)

....
....
....
....

What, if anything, do you find difficult about taking notes?

....
....
....
....

How useful to you are the notes you currently take? Can you make sense of them when you look back at them later? Can you use them for the intended purpose?

....
....

Approaching note-taking

> "My notes end up being longer than the original source!"

Have you identified anything you find difficult about note-taking? Note-taking is a skill that requires practice and many students aren't specifically taught how to take notes. There can be additional difficulties for some neurodivergent students. Some of the most common difficulties can include:

- not being able to distinguish between the important information to note down and the less important information that can be ignored
- trying to write down everything that's being said rather than just the key points of a talk or text
- not being able to write or type notes quickly enough to keep up, particularly in live lectures or in class
- difficulties understanding and processing the information from a lecture at the same time as writing notes
- being unable to make sense of notes made when later using them.

> "I want to make notes but can't concentrate on the content of the lecture if I'm concentrating on making notes. I come out not having understood and with notes that don't make sense. I understand better without making notes."

READING AND NOTE-TAKING

Notes are for your personal use, so, as long as they make sense to you and you can use them for what you need them for, there is no "right" or "wrong" way of taking notes. As always, the best way is the way that works for you. Although there's no "right" way of taking notes, some general questions to ask yourself can include:

Do you really need to take notes as you listen?

First, check you actually need to take notes. If you're given handouts or the lecture is recorded, it might not be essential to take extensive notes. Highlighting or annotating key points on the handouts might be sufficient. Listening with your full attention might be beneficial if you think you'd learn and remember more that way. If you're watching a video recording of a lecture, don't forget to pause at regular intervals to make notes rather than trying to listen and make notes simultaneously if you find that difficult.

How do you prefer to take notes?

What do you find easiest and quickest – making handwritten notes, or typing them? Try both ways. Some people find they remember more from physically writing rather than typing. Others prefer the ease of typed notes. Some people are easily distracted by notifications or apps when typing notes on a laptop or tablet, so prefer handwriting notes to avoid distractions. The best way is whatever works for you at the time.

Would note-taking software help you?

Some students, particularly those who are neurodivergent or have a disability, benefit from note-taking software. Some programs transcribe lectures and combine the transcription with slides and your notes. Ask your college or university what's available to you. And, if you are using software, take the time to learn how to use it effectively so that it becomes something that helps rather than hinders.

Are you confusing transcribing with note-taking?

Making notes should not be confused with making a transcription (a word-for-word record). Notes are key words or information you need. You don't have to use full sentences, correct spelling or punctuation. You can make bullet lists, mind-maps, diagrams or whatever works for you. You can use abbreviations, symbols, arrows or anything that helps.

Are you keeping it simple?
Colour-coding and other methods can help some students, but ensure this doesn't become time consuming or take your focus away from the content.

Are you able to use your notes?
There's no point making notes if you're not able to use them. Make notes with your purpose in mind – do you need the information to revise from for an exam, or to write an assignment about? Keep your notes accessible and organized. You might choose to organize them by theme or topic, either digitally or in a paper file.

Are you picking out the key information?
The information you'll need to note down will differ depending on where and why you're taking notes. Sometimes you might be given specific questions to answer about something you're reading or watching. In these cases, it's helpful to read the questions first so that you know what you're looking for.

At other times, your reason for taking notes might be less specific. For example, in a lecture, you might need to make notes so you have a record of what was taught so you can use it in future assignments and examinations. Of course, if you've been given essay titles in advance, this might help you distinguish between what is most relevant for you to note down and what will be less relevant.

If you don't yet know exactly what information you'll need, what's best to note? It might be that you note down names, dates, facts and statistics – things that you might otherwise forget. You might also make a note of any further resources or reading that your lecturer mentions, so that you can find these in the future. And you might need to note the main points of a lecture (e.g. the topics and examples covered). Ensure you have enough information to make sense of it at a later date – making use of sub-headings, key words and bullet points can be helpful.

> "I make notes but don't look back at them. It would probably be helpful. I forget I have them."

Try it out! Choose an article, webinar, podcast or chapter from a textbook. The topic isn't important for this activity – it's more to practise note-taking skills. Make notes on the lines below so that you could use these notes at a later date to explain the main content of the lecture to somebody who didn't attend. Remember you can type up these activities if that's how you'd usually make notes (or try a different way and compare what feels easier).

Look back at your notes. What have you done well and not so well?

....
....
....

Consider your reflections.

Did you notice a tendency to write in full sentences?

....
....

Did you find it easy to pick out the key information – such as names, dates, statistics?

....
....

Could you use your notes in the future?

....
....

What are you going to try next time?

....
....

If you find it difficult to take notes during classes and lectures, then speak to your tutors, SENCo or Disability Advisor. Specialist note-taking software could be helpful to you, or they might be able to make other suggestions, such as ensuring tutors provide printouts of the presentation in advance for you to annotate.

Let's look at a real-life example!
Look at the following notes made by a student listening to a psychology lecture.

READING AND NOTE-TAKING

Organizational psychology is also sometimes called industrial organizational psychology and has been researched for more than a century and is an exciting field of study as workplaces, attitudes to work and workers' rights evolve. It applies psychological principles to the workplace, the world of work and organizations. So, it is about how people think, behave and interact in the workplace. ...Some of the things going to be covered in this lecture are employee wellbeing and motivation which includes things like job satisfaction, stress management and getting a work-life balance. ...Then leadership and teamwork — what makes an effective leader and what makes an effective team. Then we will look at recruitment. So how are employees recruited and selected to find the best employees for the job. Training and development is also an aspect of organizational psychology....designing training programmes to ensure employees have the right skills and perform effectively. And the last point we'll cover in today's lecture is organizational change which means...

Reading these, you can see that the student has tried to transcribe almost word-for-word exactly what the lecturer was saying. This was likely stressful for the student trying to keep up with the rate of speech and means that they probably missed some of what was being said. The student has repeated some of the lecturer's words, which won't be necessary when they come to use their notes (e.g. "the last point we'll cover in today's lecture").

Now look at these notes in comparison:

Organizational Psychology (Workplace)

- *Employee Wellbeing and Motivation*
- *Leadership and teamwork*
- *Recruitment*
- *Training and Development*
- *Organizational Change*

These notes are much shorter. The student has noted down the key points (in this case the list of topics that will be covered) using bullet points and has enough information here to be able to look back at this and understand it.

Give it another go! Try the same exercise as earlier. Choose a podcast, lecture, webinar, video or book chapter and make notes. Consider how you made notes last time and how you could improve.

READING AND NOTE-TAKING

Writing a summary

Sometimes students are asked to read an article or text and to make a summary of it in order to share this with other students at a seminar. So, what does "writing a summary" actually mean?

Writing a summary isn't simply copying out the text or reading it aloud. It's about picking out the main points, the key argument, and presenting them in a short, concise and logical way, so that other students can easily understand, even though they haven't read the article themselves.

Here is how you can go about writing a summary.

1. **Read the article carefully** and make sure you've understood it. Look back earlier in this chapter for some helpful strategies on reading.

2. **Identify the main idea.** How could you summarize the article in just one sentence? (E.g. "This article is about a research project which investigated how helpful clients found bereavement counselling.")

3. **Identify the main points.** Look at the sub-headings and sections in the article to help you do this. These will be the points you need to mention in your summary. (E.g. "The rationale for this study was…", "The method the researchers used was…", "Their main findings were…", "The conclusions the researchers came to were…")

4. **Write the summary in your own words.** Keep it short – a summary is a condensed version of a text.

5. **Use signposting to help your listener to keep track.** (E.g. "The first point covered…", "The final point covered…", "Next the researchers looked at…", "Then the author considers…")

Have a go! Choose an article or section of a textbook and try to write a summary.

....

....

....

....
....
....

What do you think you've done well? If you were given this summary do you think you'd have all the key information?

....
....
....
....

SUMMARY

In this chapter, you have learned:

- Reading and note-taking are essential aspects of studying, especially at higher levels.

- You can use different approaches to reading, depending on why you are reading. For example, focused, detailed reading is not always required. Sometimes skimming or scanning is more appropriate.

- Reading critically for academic purposes means asking questions about what you are reading. You might need to reflect on who wrote the piece and why they wrote it, whether the piece gives a balanced view, if statements are backed up with evidence, and if the evidence is from reliable sources.

- You might need to take notes in classes or when reading. The most important thing about note-taking is that you are able to use the notes for the purposes you intend. They only need to make sense to you, so you can make notes in whatever way works best for you.

Chapter 6

WRITTEN ASSIGNMENTS

> "I can't approach written assignments in the linear way expected by my tutors. My brain doesn't work like that. I have to follow my current energies and interests but I always have the bigger picture in mind. I know where I'm going. I'm just getting there a different way."

In this chapter, we consider how to plan, write and proofread written assignments. The format of written assignments will vary depending on the subject, course and level you're studying at and might include writing essays, articles, business reports, writing up experiments, or longer dissertations.

 Consider the feedback you've had for written assignments in the past. What are your strengths?

....
....
....
....
....

And what would you like to improve at?

．．．

．．．

．．．

．．．

COMMON DIFFICULTIES

Academic writing can seem difficult, especially when you're new to studying at higher levels, but it's a skill you'll improve at with practice.

Some common difficulties for students include:

- not answering the question that is being asked
- putting irrelevant information in your answer
- producing an assignment that is too long or too short
- producing writing that doesn't flow coherently
- writing in a chatty rather than a formal style
- incorrect referencing
- copying directly from other sources (plagiarism)
- not checking the completed essay for spelling, punctuation or grammatical errors.

> "I find open-ended essay questions overwhelming. Where to start? Where to end? What to include?"

In addition, if you're neurodivergent, you'll likely find this affects your written work. For example, if you find it difficult to concentrate, focus, plan ahead or organize your thoughts, this will affect written work as well as other aspects of life. You might find that overthinking, procrastination or perfectionist traits get in the way. And some neurodivergent students have difficulty understanding what the question is asking or staying on topic.

> "I struggle to 'read between the lines'. Questions that ask me to pick out characters' feelings, emotions or motives are really difficult."

Have you already learnt anything about yourself from previous chapters that will help you when planning or writing your assignments? (E.g. time management strategies that work for you.)

....
....
....
....
....

Understanding the assignment

Before you write, or even plan, a written assignment, you need to understand what's being asked. You might write an absolutely brilliant essay but, if you've not answered the question that was set, you won't get any marks at all.

What to look for:

1. Identify **the format** required – do you need to write an essay, a report, a newspaper article etc? This will determine how you structure your piece and the style you write in.

2. Identify **the command words** (see the list below) – have you been asked to describe something, compare, explain, analyse or evaluate etc? This will determine the points you need to include and how you need to develop each point.

3. Note **the word count** – is there a maximum? How much can you go over or under without being penalized?

4. Look for **any other information** in the assignment brief – are you given certain topics or sub-points to include? Do you have to use case studies, statistics, your own research, quotations, references etc? Have you been given a mark scheme or assessment criteria so you can see what you're being assessed against?

Command words

Command words are the words that tell you what to do in a task or question. Different command words require different responses. Some examples of common command words and their meanings are below.

Apply	Link existing knowledge to a new situation or example.
Analyse	Break the subject down into separate parts and examine each. Show how ideas are related and why they are important.
Compare	Examine the subjects in detail, considering similarities and differences.
Consider	Think carefully and write about the subject from different perspectives.
Critically compare	Compare and consider the positive aspects and limitations of the subject.
Demonstrate	Show an understanding by describing, explaining or illustrating using examples.
Describe	Write about the subject giving detailed information in a logical way.
Develop	Expand a plan or idea by adding more detail or depth of information.
Differentiate	Identify the differences between two or more things.
Discuss	Write a detailed account giving a range of views or opinions.

WRITTEN ASSIGNMENTS

Evaluate	Examine strengths, weaknesses, arguments for and against, similarities and differences. Judge evidence from different perspectives and make a valid conclusion or reasoned judgement.
Explain	Provide detailed information about the subject with reasons or examples showing how or why.
Identify	Recognize and name the main points.
Implement	Explain how to put an idea or plan into action.
Plan	Think about and organize information in a sensible way.
Show	Give evidence to demonstrate knowledge and understanding.
Summarize	Give the main ideas or facts in a concise way.

Here's an exercise to show how different command words require different answers.

Choose a book (or television show, movie, computer game etc) and answer the following questions about it. It doesn't really matter what you choose, the idea is to practise answering in different ways.

Identify the main points (of the book).

....
....
....
....
....

Summarize (the book).

....
....
....
....
....

Compare (the book) with (another book).

....
....
....
....
....

Discuss how (the book) approaches its topic.

....
....
....
....
....

Describe a character (from the book).

....
....
....
....
....

Explain why a character acts the way that they do.

....
....
....
....
....

Evaluate the character's actions throughout (the book).

....
....
....
....
....

You'll have realized that your answers to these questions are all slightly different even though you're writing about the same thing. It's really important to identify the command words in your academic assignments to ensure you're including what's required in your answers.

Planning and structuring

Once you understand what the assignment is asking you to do, it's time to plan what to include and consider how best to structure your answer.

Planner or pantser?

Writers often describe themselves as planners or pantsers. Are you someone who plans every detail of your work and sticks to your plan exactly? Or do you write your essays "by the seat of your pants" (without a plan or outline, you just write spontaneously)?

 Are you a planner or a pantser? How do you think this helps and / or hinders you?

....
....
....
....

There's no right or wrong way to approach writing – going with your natural inclinations can often be most effective, but it's also worth considering what could help you make the process easier.

Planning can help ensure you include everything that you need to and can help you include it in a logical order. It makes the writing process easier for a lot of people.

But sticking too rigidly to a plan might mean you don't respond flexibly to your thoughts and understanding that develops during the researching and writing processes. Try a few different approaches and see what works best for you.

WRITTEN ASSIGNMENTS

Gathering ideas

> "Mind-maps don't work for me. I need something more linear."

What helps you gather ideas for an assignment? Do you make a mind-map, a list, use a planning frame etc? What else could you try?

....

....

....

....

Some students like to mind-map their ideas. This simply means writing the title in the centre of a page and drawing arrows to the points you'd like to make. You can then add sub-points or arrows to link ideas. An example of a mind-map on "Study Skills" is here:

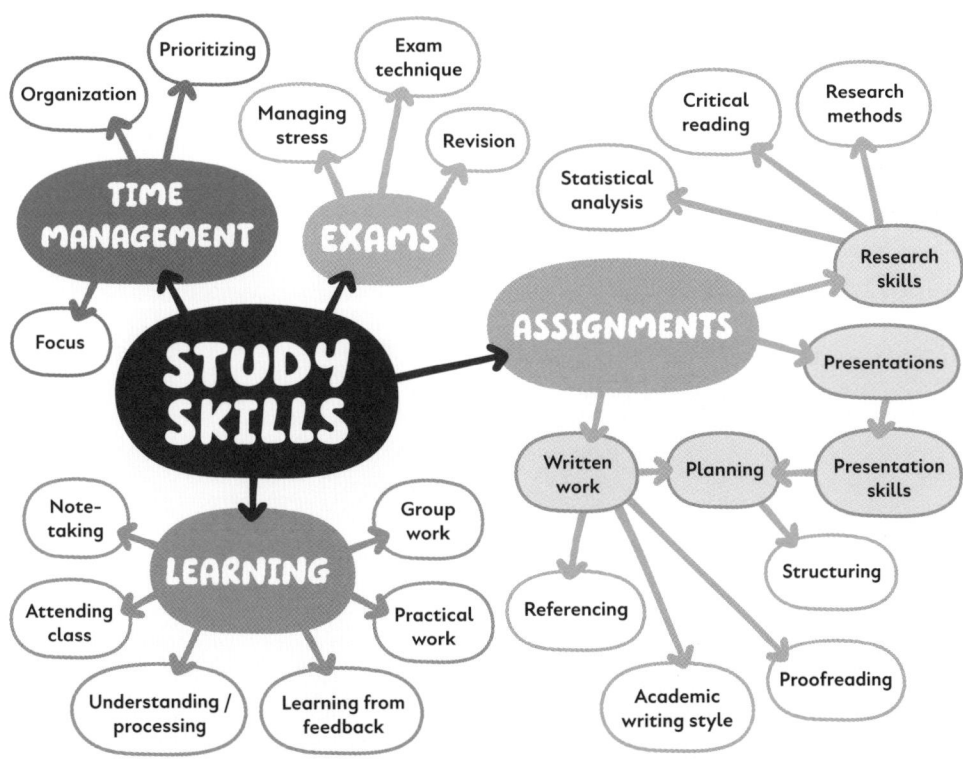

Mind-mapping software is also available which allows users to move ideas around on the screen. Once you've made a mind-map you can refer to your notes, textbooks, journal articles or other research to fill in any gaps or add more detail.

If you don't find mind-maps helpful, you could try other ways of gathering ideas. Some students like to make a list of bullet points; others prefer to write each idea on a sticky note which they can then move around to order their points. Try out a few ways and see what works best for you. Whatever strategy you use, this stage is about gathering ideas. It gives you an indication of what you'd like to include, and helps you identify what you still need to find out. This gathering of ideas and "thinking time" helps you to ensure you include what is required and that you don't miss anything.

Considering the structure

Once you've decided what to include, you need to decide **how** to structure the information so you present it in a logical order that makes sense. Putting your ideas in a logical order makes it much easier for the reader to follow your arguments and your reasoning. The process of gathering ideas and considering how to structure them also supports your own understanding of the topic. You'll be considering how points are linked to each other and will be considering the wider context of your arguments.

Some assignments have clear instructions about how to structure the piece. For example, a write-up of a science experiment would usually require certain sections in a set order:

1. Introduction
2. Hypothesis
3. Materials
4. Method
5. Results
6. Discussion
7. Conclusion.

WRITTEN ASSIGNMENTS

If you're not given a set structure, you might need to consider the structure yourself.

On a basic level, most assignments usually require:

1. **An introduction** – where you set out the topic you'll cover and arguments you'll make.

2. **The main body** – split into several paragraphs:
   - Each main point you make should be discussed in a separate paragraph, or split into several paragraphs.
   - These paragraphs should be presented in a logical order so that the essay flows and does not jump from topic to topic.

3. **A conclusion** – where you summarize your discussion and come to any conclusions.

The following is a template you could use to plan the structure of the assignment. You could make bullet points or notes in each box to remind yourself of the points you'll include when you come to writing up the assignment.

You might need to adapt this template so that it makes sense for the assignment you are undertaking, and some of the structures that follow might work better for the assignment you're completing.

FINDING JOY IN STUDYING

Essay Template #1

Introduction:

Paragraph 1:

Paragraph 2:

Paragraph 3:

Paragraph 4:

Conclusion:

WRITTEN ASSIGNMENTS

 An essay in which you have to present a balanced argument

Essay Template

Introduction:

Background to the topic:

Arguments FOR:

Arguments AGAINST:

Conclusion:

FINDING JOY IN STUDYING

 An essay in which you have to compare two topics or issues

Essay Template #3

Introduction:

Similarities:

Differences:

Conclusion:

WRITTEN ASSIGNMENTS

 A research report

Essay Template #4

Abstract:

Introduction:

Lit. review/previous research:

Methodology:

Results/findings:

Discussion:

Conclusion:

References:

A business report

Essay Template #5

Executive summary:

Table of contents:

Introduction:

Methodology:

Findings:

Discussion:

Conclusion:

Appendices:

WRITTEN ASSIGNMENTS

Always check for the exact requirements of each assignment – your college or university might require different sections than the sample templates given here.

ACADEMIC WRITING SKILLS

> "I find writing absolutely tortuous. But I've learned to get something down – even if the sentences are simple and repetitive – I just have to get it down. Once I've got something the process seems so much easier. I can edit it and improve it. I've got something to work with then and that's so much easier than a blank page."

Academic essays are usually written in a specific style. Tick or circle which answer you think applies:

Academic writing is:	Formal	or	informal?
	Biased	or	impartial?
	Personal	or	impersonal?
	Precise	or	vague?

Academic writing is formal, impartial, impersonal and precise:

- Language should be formal rather than chatty – avoid slang words and contractions (e.g. use *cannot* rather than *can't*).

- Writing should be impartial – statements should be based on evidence and both sides of an argument considered.

- Personal opinions (e.g. "I like..." and "In my opinion...") are usually avoided in academic writing unless in personal reflection pieces.

- Academic writing aims to be precise. So, rather than a statement such as "Ages ago, someone pointed out that...", use "In 1997, research by Smith and Johnson suggested that...".

Academic writing can seem tricky at first but often becomes easier over time.

> Look at these examples. Which do you think would be suitable in an academic essay, and which less suitable?
>
> 1. This evidence suggests that…
> 2. Evidence that supports this theory includes…
> 3. I don't agree with the current political system.
> 4. On the other hand, opponents of this theory claim…
> 5. Some research shows that this is not true.
> 6. Most people dislike going to the supermarket.
> 7. People have played tennis for a long time.
> 8. A 2022 research study by Smith *et al.* indicated that…

Let's take a look at each of the examples.

1. Suitable for inclusion in an academic essay.
2. Suitable for inclusion in an academic essay.
3. This is a personal opinion and less suitable for an academic essay.
4. Suitable for inclusion in an academic essay.
5. This is vague (which research shows this?).
6. This example is a generalization and vague (is there any research evidence to prove this?).

7. This example is also vague (how long and which people where?).

8. Suitable for inclusion in an academic essay.

Signposting

When you're writing an academic essay it's important to present your ideas in a logical order and link them together. This makes it much easier for the reader to follow your arguments and is sometimes called "signposting" – you're giving your reader an indication of which way they are going and what is coming up next. The language you use throughout your essay can help to guide your reader in this way and shows how your thoughts link together.

As you practise writing, you'll come up with your own words and phrases, but a list of some useful "signposting" phrases is included below to get you started.

Useful phrases for academic work

Introducing new points / ideas

- First / Second / Third / Finally...
- With regards to...
- One aspect of (x) is...
- The next argument to make is...
- An important factor is...

Adding related ideas

- In addition...
- An additional point to make...
- A further argument for this is...
- Furthermore...
- Similarly...
- Moreover...
- As a consequence / Consequently...
- Another factor to take into consideration is...

Linking to different points

- Of equal importance is...
- A different perspective is that of...
- It is also important to consider...

Linking to opposing ideas

- However...
- Alternatively...
- Opponents of this theory, however, claim that...
- Nonetheless...
- An alternative perspective is...
- In comparison...

Referring to research and evidence

- Smith (2025) suggests that...
- A research study by Smith (2025) suggests that...
- Smith (2025) claims that "...".
- A 2025 study by Smith *et al.* showed that...
- This is illustrated by...
- This is consistent with the theory of..., as proposed by Smith (2025).

Coming to conclusions

- In conclusion / To conclude...
- To summarize / In summary...
- The evidence / finding suggests / indicates...
- This report has considered...
- Taking into account the evidence discussed in this report...
- This project sought to answer the question...

REFERENCING

Academic writing must be referenced accurately. Referencing means acknowledging where you found the information that you are referring to. Correct referencing also ensures that a reader can find any information you refer to for themselves.

> **Note:** There are different referencing systems and styles (e.g. Harvard, Chicago, MHRA). Check which one your college or university expects.

When you quote somebody else's words or refer to their research, you'll need to reference this. You'll often be required to include a citation within the text and then the full reference in a footnote, reference list or bibliography.

> **Tip!** Get into the habit of noting down the books or articles you use and bookmark the webpages you use. That way it'll be much quicker to add in your references. You'll need to note: name(s) of author(s), the title of the article or book, the year of publication, the publishers and the place of publication. If you're referencing a journal article you'll also need the journal title, volume number and page numbers of the article. If you're referring to something you've found on the Internet you'll also need the URL and to note the date you accessed it.

The Harvard referencing system

We are going to discuss the Harvard referencing system because it is the one that is used at most UK universities, but always check with your university which style they expect you to use and ask if they have referencing guidelines available for you to refer to.

Here is an example of how the Harvard referencing system works:

In the Harvard system, the citation within the text would include **the author's surname and the year of publication.** For example, in your essay, you might write:

> Honeybourne (2025) states: "When you quote somebody else's words or refer to their research, you'll need to reference this."
>
> Then, for the Harvard system, you'll also need to compile a reference list at the end of your assignment. This list contains the full details of the sources you have cited. These are listed in alphabetical order of the authors' surnames. For example:
>
> Honeybourne, V. (2025) *Finding Joy in Studying: An Autistic and ADHD Guide to Uncovering the Study Skills that Work for You.* London, UK: Jessica Kingsley Publishers.

In some systems, a bibliography rather than a reference list will be required. A bibliography is a list of materials you have used when researching the subject, but not necessarily cited.

 Do a little research:

What system does your college or university expect you to use?

....
....

How would you reference a book source using this system?

....
....
....
....
....
....
....
....

How would you reference a journal article using this system?

....
....
....
....
....
....
....
....

How would you reference a webpage using this system?

....
....
....
....
....

Where could you get support with referencing? Have you found any useful guides or websites? Does your university have an academic support department?

....
....
....
....
....

Copying, cheating and plagiarism

What do you think counts as cheating, copying or plagiarism in academic contexts?

....
....
....
....
....
....
....

Cheating and copying others' work (plagiarism) is taken seriously in academic contexts. If accused of plagiarism, you might lose marks, be required to re-do an assignment, or be excluded altogether from the module or course. Cheating can take many forms and includes:

- copying all or parts of another student's assignment
- copying from another student in an exam
- accessing or taking prohibited materials into a controlled conditions exam
- copying directly from a book, article, website or other source in an assignment and not referencing this
- asking someone else to do the work for you
- passing off somebody else's work as your own
- changing a few words or rearranging the sentences and then passing work off as your own
- using generative AI to write all or part of an assignment for you.

Have you ever tried to write something in your own words but then worried it didn't sound good enough? You're not the only one! Many students feel this way; however, it's really important not to be tempted to copy from another source.

Try not to compare yourself to others who appear to express themselves more eloquently – not only will you avoid accusations of plagiarism, but expressing something you've learned in your own words shows your tutor what you've understood and helps them to give you constructive feedback. Schools and universities use powerful software which can detect plagiarism, so it's definitely not worth taking the risk.

If you find it difficult to write in your own words, you could try some of the following strategies to practise this skill.

- Imagine you're talking to a friend and want to explain to them what you've just read. Explain it using vocabulary that makes sense to you, without looking at the original text. This is putting something "in your own words".

- Make notes from the original text – just short bullet points or key words. Now, using just these notes, and without looking back at the original text, put these key words into your own sentences.

- Some students find they express themselves better when the process of writing doesn't get in the way. Try using voice-text dictation software and see if this helps you "use your own words".

- Alternatively, you could try presenting the original text in a different format. For example, turn the information into a flow chart, diagram or comic strip. Now use this, without the original text, to put the information in your own words. This should prevent you from looking back and lifting entire sentences.

EDITING AND PROOFREADING STRATEGIES

> "Listening to my writing was a game-changer. I hear all the errors I miss when I just try to look at the screen."

After writing comes proofreading. Proofreading involves:

- checking for typos, predictive text mistakes and spelling errors
- ensuring you've used punctuation and grammar accurately to convey your meaning
- checking your overall structure and content.

It's an opportunity to correct any errors, check you've not missed anything and improve sections that need work.

What do you notice when you proofread your work? What do you pick up most often (e.g. typos, repetition of phrases)?

....
....
....
....
....

So, how do you go about proofreading or editing? Again, this is about trying out different strategies and finding out what's most effective for you. Reflect on which of these strategies might work for you:

- **Print out your work** and proofread on paper rather than on screen.
- **Change the background colour** or font size and colour before proofreading.

- **Read your work aloud** to identify any errors.

- **Use a screen-reader** to read work aloud to you. Some students find it easier to "hear" errors rather than see them.

- **Use a spelling, punctuation and grammar checker** in the application you're writing in (e.g. Word/Pages/Google Docs etc) to identify errors and suggest replacements.
  - Be aware that these do not always pick up errors such as typos or incorrect predictive text choices! For example, if you meant to type "copy" but typed "cope" instead, spell checker won't pick this up as an error.

- **Use a thesaurus and dictionary** (either paper or online) to check spellings, word choice and meanings.

- **Leave a few days between writing and proofreading** to help you see if your writing still makes sense.

- **Try not to proofread when you're tired.** If we're tired our brains are less likely to see the mistakes and will "fill in the gaps" for us.

Proofreading might seem a bit of a boring task – after all, you've already written the piece – but it can actually make a huge difference. A good edit and proofread can turn an average essay into a great essay!

So, what sorts of things do you need to look for when it comes to editing and proofreading your work? On the next page is a downloadable checklist for you to use every time you have an assignment.

WRITTEN ASSIGNMENTS

Proofreading checklist. Have you checked...

- Spelling, including typos and incorrect choices made by predictive text? ☐

- Punctuation such as full stops, commas, capital letters and apostrophes? ☐

- Word choices? Does your essay use formal, academic vocabulary? Have you avoided slang words? ☐

- Each sentence is clear and makes sense? ☐

- You've included a clear introduction and a logical conclusion? ☐

- You've split your work up into clear paragraphs or sections that are all in a logical order? ☐

- You've signposted your reader through your essay with headlines, useful phrases or linking sentences appropriately? ☐

- The points you made are backed up with evidence? ☐

- You've referenced research and quotes accurately in the text, and in the reference list? ☐

- You've avoided repeating the same ideas or points? ☐

- You've answered the question, and that each point you make is relevant? ☐

- You're within the word limit? ☐

- You've read the assignment brief to ensure you've included everything necessary? ☐

- You've looked at any specific guidence your college or university has provided in terms of how to present assignments? ☐

Spelling, punctuation and grammar

When writing for academic purposes you should try to use correct spelling, punctuation and grammar. If you're less confident using correct spelling, punctuation and grammar you might feel that academic writing isn't for you – but don't let it put you off studying! These are skills that can be improved with practice. Some possible ideas to help with spelling, punctuation and grammar are listed below:

- Try to attend modules or workshops in academic writing skills if your school or university offers one.

- Seek out study skills specialists who might be able to offer individualized advice if you have access to one-to-one support.

- Don't let a lack of confidence in your spelling, punctuation or grammar get in the way of your writing!

- See it as a two-step process.
    - First, concentrate on getting your ideas down in the first instance.
    - Then, concentrate on checking for spelling or punctuation when proofreading.

- Try dictating a first draft using the voice-to-text function so you don't have to worry about spelling when writing.

- Think when using spellchecking software onscreen – don't just click on the first alternative unless you're sure it's correct. Take a moment to read a definition too.

- Use an onscreen spelling, punctuation and grammar checker as a starting point. It's always worth reading over it yourself – it might not have picked up on typos or missing words, for example.

- Use your essay plan to split your work into paragraphs and sort out a logical order before you begin. It can be easier than having to go back afterwards and split up a longer text or move things around.

- Keep it simple. It can be tempting to want to use long, impressive-sounding academic sentences, but it's more important that you make sense. Use short, clear sentences that make sense.

RECEIVING FEEDBACK

> "I get so demoralized reading feedback from my tutors. It always sounds so critical. I feel so embarrassed."

Feedback – what is it and why does it matter?

When studying, you'll receive feedback from your tutors on the work you submit. Effective feedback:

- tells you what you've done well
- tells you what you've done less well
- identifies any misunderstandings
- explains clearly how you can improve your work next time.

> "Feedback such as 'You might like to look at the research of so-and-so' isn't clear enough for me. Do I need to, or don't I?"

Hopefully, the feedback you receive will be clear and help you improve your future work. Receiving useful feedback is a really helpful tool for developing both your subject knowledge and as a learner. But sometimes students can feel feedback is confusing, vague, unhelpful or unfair.

Coping with feedback

Focus on the positives

First, it's easy to disregard positive feedback. As humans we often experience what's called "Negative Cognitive Bias". This means we tend to notice and remember the negatives more than the positives, even when the positives outnumber the negatives. So, when receiving feedback on your work, do remember to take in the positives! Pay attention to what you've done well or improved at and do the same in future assignments. Make a conscious effort to note these positives, as your brain might naturally jump to anything a little more critical.

Feedback is an opportunity to learn

Teachers and tutors give feedback to help you to improve in the future. It's their job to tell you what you've done less well and how to improve. Although it can be demoralizing sometimes to read a list of improvements when you've worked really hard on a piece, it is an opportunity to learn. Remind yourself it is constructive criticism and use this to improve on future assignments.

Emotions can impact on how you take on board feedback

If you know you're sensitive to criticism, you might find it helps to wait until you're feeling in a more positive mood before you read any feedback. If you're having a day that you feel tired, stressed or down, you might be even more likely to interpret feedback more negatively or critically than it is intended.

Seek support if you don't understand

If you don't understand what the feedback means, ask for help to understand this. Ask your tutor to clarify if it doesn't make sense to you, or see if a mentor, study skills specialist or fellow student can help you to interpret it.

Make your needs known

If you're struggling to understand feedback due to your neurodivergence, speak to your tutor, SENCo or Disability Advisor. Some students have difficulty "reading between the lines" or picking up on inferred meaning, for example, and this is something that tutors could be advised about.

Peer feedback

Sometimes you might be required to engage in "peer feedback". This is where you are asked to read or watch another student's work and give them feedback on it. They will then do the same for your work. It can be a useful way of sharing ideas, seeing how other students are approaching tasks and receiving feedback on your own work. Of course, there are some limitations too. Some students are better than others at giving feedback. Some might dislike saying anything that could be perceived as critical, so they only mention the positives, meaning that the process isn't useful in helping you to identify mistakes, misunderstandings or ways to improve. Others might come across as overly critical, which can be demoralizing. And others might have misunderstood the topic, task or assessment criteria themselves, and so might inadvertently point you in the wrong direction or encourage you to change something that was fine how it was.

Here is some guidance about how to participate in peer feedback effectively:

Giving feedback

- Always remember to include some positives! Tell others what they've done well, what you enjoyed, what they've improved at or what you found interesting.

- Use any guidelines you've been given from your teacher or tutor. What have you been asked to comment on? Have you been given assessment criteria to look at?

- Try to make your feedback clear and useful.
    - For example: "I found it difficult to understand your second paragraph" is more helpful than "There were some bits I couldn't understand".

- If something is a personal preference rather than a necessary academic point, make it clear.

- If you really don't feel able to give useful feedback then say so. It's better than making a guess and potentially giving another student unhelpful feedback.

Receiving feedback

- Ask for clarity. If feedback from others is vague or you don't understand it, ask them for a specific example or to explain it differently.

- Use your judgement. Peer feedback can be useful, but do remember that other students are not experts themselves. If others say things you don't agree with, you don't have to take these onboard and make huge changes to your work – do take others' comments into consideration but use your own knowledge and judgement. Some students will be better than others at giving useful feedback.

Rejection sensitivity dysphoria and feedback

Rejection sensitivity dysphoria is a term used to describe the severe emotional pain that some people experience when they perceive (or do experience) rejection, criticism or failure of some sort. It isn't an official medical diagnosis, and it's only recently started to be researched, but it's thought to be linked to conditions in which individuals have differences in how they experience and regulate their emotions, such as ADHD and autism.

Although feeling rejected or criticized isn't something most people like, in individuals with rejection sensitivity dysphoria, these feelings are much more intense, painful and long-lasting. Individuals with rejection sensitivity dysphoria might also experience extreme anxiety even before any potential rejection or criticism, causing them to avoid the situation in advance. People affected can often interpret neutral or vague responses as highly critical.

If this affects you, it can be useful to be aware of this, as you might be more likely to react negatively to feedback when studying, perhaps interpreting it far more critically than it was actually intended. Speaking to a counsellor, therapist or specialist mentor can also be useful to help you manage these situations.

ACTION PLAN!

What actions do you need to take to help you improve your written assignments?

For example:

- Research the referencing system required.
- Brush up on your punctuation.

WRITTEN ASSIGNMENTS

- Try out some different ways of proofreading etc.

Write down anything else that you think would be most useful to you:

....
....
....
....
....

How are you going to get these actions done?

Think about how your brain works and what will realistically work for you. If you're unlikely to focus by yourself on learning how to use a referencing system, will you find it more useful to book yourself into a workshop run by your university? If you're going to refresh your knowledge of punctuation, what will work best for you and when will you get this done?

I will...

....
....
....
....
....
....
....
....
....
....

SUMMARY

This chapter has covered the planning, structuring, writing and checking of written assignments. You've learned:

- Command words in an assignment question indicate how you should approach the topic and what you need to include in your answer – pay close attention to these!

- Planning an essay before you begin to write can help ensure you don't leave out anything important and can also make the writing process easier.

- You'll need to consider how to structure your assignment. Presenting the information in a logical order makes it much easier for the reader to understand.

- Academic writing expects a certain style: formal, precise language in full sentences, usually taking an impersonal and impartial point of view.

- Academic writing requires you to reference information from other sources. Not doing this is called plagiarism (cheating).

- Proofreading your work can make a huge difference! It's a chance to spot any errors both in terms of content and language.

Chapter 7

PRESENTATION SKILLS

> "Being dyslexic, I express myself much better in presentations than on paper."

Sometimes you might be required to give a presentation – either face-to-face to tutors or peers, or videoed to be sent to tutors for marking. Giving an oral presentation can be nerve-racking for some.

In this chapter we'll look at how to **plan**, **prepare** and **deliver presentations**, as well as reducing anxiety around presentations.

WHAT MAKES A GOOD PRESENTATION?

Think back to a presentation, talk or lecture you heard that was really effective. Why did it make such an impact?

....

....

....

....

....

What do you think? Maybe you identified that the presenter was very enthusiastic or knowledgeable about their subject, used humour, or explained everything really clearly. Or perhaps the speaker used relevant video clips, diagrams or examples which really helped the audience to understand and feel engaged. Perhaps the presentation was very well structured and easy to follow.

Now consider a presentation, talk or lecture you've heard that was ineffective or boring. Why do you think this was?

. . . .

. . . .

. . . .

. . . .

. . . .

. . . .

. . . .

Let's reflect on your answers. There might have been various reasons you considered a presentation to be unsuccessful. Maybe you simply weren't interested in the subject matter, or the information was nothing new to you. Perhaps you didn't understand the topic or you weren't in the right frame of mind to take in new information – you were tired or worried about something. Maybe the presenter came across as too nervous, quiet or unenthusiastic. You might have identified a practical or environmental reason why you couldn't engage – for example, the room was overheated or overcrowded, you couldn't hear the presenter, you couldn't see the slides from where you were sitting, your chair was uncomfortable, you were distracted by something outside, there was technological failure or frequent interruptions.

You can't control all these factors when presenting, especially in a studying context, when you often have little say over the physical environment and have to meet a strict set of criteria of what to include. But there are other aspects that you do have influence over – and these are what we'll focus on in this chapter. But first, let's look at any presenting you have already done and reflect on this.

How do you currently feel about giving presentations? Does the format (e.g. face-to-face or videoed) make a difference?

....
....
....
....
....
....

Consider all types of "talks" (presentations, meetings, speeches at a party). Have you ever given a talk or presentation that went well? Why was this?

....
....
....
....
....
....

What would you like to improve at in terms of presentation skills?

....
....
....
....
....
....

Be realistic in what you'd like to achieve. If public speaking isn't your thing, a goal such as looking up from your notes from time to time, speaking a little more loudly or pausing after each sentence to slow down might be a good place to start.

COMMON DIFFICULTIES WITH PRESENTATIONS

> "I dread presentations. The anxiety is overwhelming."

Many people say that public speaking is something that creates feelings of anxiety, so if you fall into this category you're certainly not alone. Often you might find that nerves mean you don't come across as confidently as you'd like, or that being "put on the spot" means you feel anxious, forget things you'd like to say or even rush to get the ordeal finished as quickly as you can. If you're neurodivergent, you might have some specific difficulties with presentations.

Social anxiety
People with difficulties relating to social anxiety might find public speaking especially hard, having to "perform" in public and having people looking and listening to you.

Verbal and non-verbal communication
If you find eye contact uncomfortable you might dislike being in front of an audience. Or, you might find it difficult to change your facial expression or tone of voice when you're concentrating on remembering what to say. Some people worry that stimming, fidgeting or differences in their body language can also affect their confidence when giving presentations.

Sensitivity to criticism
Putting yourself "out there" in front of people can be especially scary if you feel they are judging you or going to be critical. Some neurodivergent

individuals might be particularly sensitive to criticism (this is sometimes called "rejection sensitivity dysphoria" and is discussed in Chapter 6).

Although there may be difficulties, many neurodivergent individuals do enjoy public speaking, and others do learn to get better at it. Let's look at some reasons neurodivergent students gave for liking public speaking:

- They feel they express themselves much better through speech than through writing – especially dyslexic students.
- Some feel their personality comes through in person much better than on paper.
- Some are extroverts and enjoy the face-to-face interaction with others – this might be especially true if you're an ADHDer.
- Some find the one-way communication of giving a presentation much easier than the group dynamics of general conversation.

So, don't assume you won't be good at presentations just because you're neurodivergent. Everyone has individual strengths and difficulties – there might be some aspects you're good at, some you will improve at, and other aspects you find difficult.

> "I actually like giving presentations now my confidence has improved. Speaking to a group of people saying something I've prepared is so much easier than taking part in an unpredictable conversation or class discussion."

As with many tasks, even if you have difficulties, the first step in addressing these difficulties and feeling less nervous is to be prepared. In the next section we will consider what this entails.

PREPARING FOR A PRESENTATION

Before preparing your presentation, confirm the details. Every time you have a presentation, write down and answer each of the questions below.

- Is the presentation in person, live online or recorded in advance?
- How long do you have to speak for?
- Location (if in person)?
- Platform used (if online)?
- Who's the audience?
- Visual support required (e.g. slides)?
- Any other requirements (e.g. Q&A session, audience participation, handouts)?
- Am I clear on what to include? (Look at the assessment criteria and brief as you would with any assignment.)

Research

You'll likely need to research your topic before preparing your presentation. Research skills are the same whether for a written or spoken assignment, so go back to Chapter 5: "Reading and Note-Taking" for some ideas of how to do this. Also remember to include references in your presentation if this is required.

PRESENTATION SKILLS

Structure

As with written assignments, a well-structured presentation is much easier for the audience, and assessor, to follow.

Presentation structure

Introduction:

Tell your audience:
- what you'll be talking about
- the angle you're taking or argument you're making
- the topics or points you'll cover.

A contents slide can be useful and anything else you think is important for the audience to know at the relevant points (such as if you'll be taking questions at the end).

Main:

- Make your points in a logical order.
- How much detail you go into depends on the length of the presentation.
- Use research studies, case studies, references or examples to back up your points if necessary.
- Explain any specialist terminology if necessary.

Conclusion:

Bring it all together in your conclusion. Summarize what you've covered and the arguments you've made, share your reference list (or further resources) if required, and take questions if required.

You might find it useful to look back at Chapter 6: "Written Assignments" for other ways of structuring a piece of work. For example, depending on your presentation, you might need to structure it in one of the following ways:

FINDING JOY IN STUDYING

 Looking at both sides of an argument

Essay Template

Introduction:

Background to the topic:

Arguments FOR:

Arguments AGAINST:

Conclusion:

PRESENTATION SKILLS

 Presenting a research project or case study

Essay Template

Introduction:

Background:

Lit. review:

Methodology:

Results:

Discussion:

Conclusions:

Using a template, mind-map or other visual structure can be a useful starting point once you've done your research. Make some brief notes in each section of the points you want to cover.

Visual support

A presentation might require visual support such as a slideshow.

What do you think makes effective visual support?

....

....

....

You might have identified aspects such as:

- use of a clear font, large enough to be read by the audience
- a neutral background that enables the text to be read easily
- titles on slides
- a contents slide at the beginning
- photos, pictures or diagrams that are relevant to what is being said
- key points displayed only – not the entire script of what is being said.

Tip! It can be easy to waste time creating a slideshow with graphics and animations, but usually, it's the content that's assessed, not the design. Focus on the content first.

Once you've planned, researched and considered the structure for your presentation, you might then decide to create your slideshow (if one is required). Check if your tutors have given any guidance about what to include in your slideshow beforehand.

Design your slideshow with your audience in mind. Is the text large enough and easy to read? Are any pictures or diagrams large and clear enough? Are you giving them too much to read on each slide? Generally, the slideshow should back up what you, the presenter, are saying. It can be confusing for the audience if they are reading something on a slide and you are talking about something else, and it's usually unnecessary for them to simply read a word-for-word transcription of what you are saying. If you're reading a slide aloud, that's also likely to be less interesting than you speaking naturally about the topic, picture or diagram. An effective slideshow can help the audience to understand what you're talking about and can help you to remember what you want to say and in which order.

Rehearsing

Many people find it's helpful to rehearse their presentation. It can help you feel more confident on the day and helps to sort out any practical issues, such as ensuring you can stick to the time limit. Rehearsing a presentation doesn't usually mean learning a script off by heart. Often this won't end up sounding very natural and might actually make you more stressed if you feel you've forgotten your words or what comes next. Nor should a presentation sound like an essay read aloud. Written and spoken language use different conventions. A spoken presentation will likely not sound as "academic" as a written essay. Presenting is more about talking as spontaneously as you can about prepared points. Rehearsing is a chance for you to gain confidence and order your thoughts about what you want to say rather than to learn a script word-for-word. Every time you rehearse your presentation will probably sound a bit different – and that is fine. Here are some cues for you to think about to help you determine what works best for you when you're rehearsing.

How do you like to practise?

- talking out loud to yourself
- presenting to a pet who's a good listener
- practising in front of a friend or family member
- videoing yourself and watching it back
- another way.

And what do you like to do?

- speak completely "off the cuff" – you speak like you're having a conversation, unprepared
- use your slideshow to remind you of the points to make
- make cue cards or notes to remind you of the main points
- writing up a "script" to start with, then use this less as you become more confident with the topic.

What to include in notes or cue cards?

If you're making prompts (either on cue cards, notes or your slideshow) to help you on the day, what could you include? Some people find it's enough to note down the key points or key words for each topic to jog their memory. Sometimes, you might decide to note down key statistics, names, facts or references to ensure accuracy.

Signposting

Signposting is as important in oral presentations as it is in written assignments. Signposting involves guiding the audience through your presentation, making it easier for them to understand where you're up to and to follow your arguments.

Useful phrases that aid signposting include:

- "My first / second point is…"
- "The final point I'd like to make…"
- "To illustrate my last point…"
- "An alternative view, however, is…"

Coping with nerves

If you get anxious about giving presentations, you're not alone! Many people find speaking in front of others nerve-racking, and if you're neurodivergent you might have additional differences in how you communicate and experience social situations. However, it's a skill many people do learn to become more confident about. Look at the diagram on the next double spread for some ideas.

PRESENTING SKILLS

No two people present in the same style. Often the most effective presenters are those who are confident being themselves. However, some general tips that many people find effective include the following:

- If you're presenting face-to-face, try to look at your audience from time to time rather than just looking down at your notes. This can make your presentation more engaging and helps to project your voice.

- Ensure you're speaking loudly enough so that the audience can hear. Be aware also of your speed – it can be easy to talk quickly when nervous. Pause regularly and take breaths! When you're presenting, a tiny pause can feel like a lifetime, so you might need to tell yourself not to rush.

- Be aware of where you're standing so that visuals such as your slideshow can be seen by the audience.

- Refer to your visuals so the audience knows why you're sharing the information.

- Smiling can help you feel more relaxed (even if you're just recording a voice-over for a presentation).

Consider how you present. Do you:

- fidget a lot?
- stim?
- bounce?
- use humour / sarcasm?
- move around?
- stay still?
- look down?
- use lots of gestures?

REDUCING

BREATHE
Spend a few moments before presenting by taking some deep breaths. Remember to pause for breath after each sentence too. This will ensure you don't speak too quickly, and help you feel calmer.

CONGRATULATE
Praise yourself for trying something new. Focus on what went well and what you've improved on.

STAND TALL
Standing with your feet firmly on the floor can help you feel grounded.

PRACTISE
Rehearsing can help you feel more confident. Remind yourself you know your topic.

CONSIDER YOUR NEEDS
If you feel confident enough, tell your tutors and / or audience what you find difficult (e.g. "I'm autistic and I personally find direct eye contact difficult"). This might help your audience understand why you present a certain way.

LOOK UP
Making eye contact with your audience (or pretending to – pick a spot on the wall behind them) and smiling can help you look and feel more relaxed.

NERVES

BE MINDFUL
Negative self-talk and feelings of nervousness will pass. Learning mindfulness techniques (such as meditation) might help you manage negative and uncomfortable emotions.

BE HONEST
If you forget what you were going to say, lose your place or need a moment to think about an answer, tell your audience this and take a moment to get back on track.

REALIZE
You might think things didn't go to plan, but it's likely the audience didn't notice (or won't remember) if you mixed up a few words or felt flustered.

REMIND YOURSELF
It's normal to feel nervous. Plenty of others feel the same. Feeling a little bit anxious might actually motivate you to prepare.

BE NATURAL
Try to be yourself. Imagine you are talking to a group of supporting friends. This may help you feel more relaxed.

PUT IT IN PERSPECTIVE
Your presentation is probably only a small part of your course assessment. You're often assessed on the content rather than your presentation skills.

You don't necessarily need to change your natural inclinations (unless it's necessary – for example, there might be a topic when a humorous or sarcastic approach isn't suitable), but if there is anything you feel self-conscious or worried about, you might want to consider if you'll:

- do nothing differently – just accept that is what you do
- use something that'll help you feel more comfortable or confident (e.g. a fidget toy)
- explain your needs to the audience (e.g. "I find I concentrate much better with a fidget toy, so that's why I've got one with me").

There are no right or wrong answers to this and different people will have different preferences. Just consider what might help you feel as relaxed and as confident as possible.

If the anxiety is overwhelming

Of course, there can be times for some students when the anxiety about public speaking becomes overwhelming and makes the task impossible. What you choose to do will depend on your individual needs and circumstances, but there might be several options.

Build up your skills

If you feel you could build up these skills, perhaps teachers and tutors can help you work on your skills slowly. For example, you might feel able to stand at the front with a classmate when they do the talking and you hold up a poster. The next time, you feel able to make a brief point as part of a group presentation and so on.

Speak to someone

You could speak to your tutors and explain your needs. They might be able to offer an alternative, such as you videoing a presentation and sending it to them if you feel comfortable doing that rather than a face-to-face presentation.

Alternatively, you could speak to your SENCo or Disability Advisor who will be able to advocate and approach subject tutors for you.

PRESENTATION SKILLS

If you experience social anxiety which negatively impacts your life, speak to a counsellor or therapist for specialist support.

Presentations – Bringing it all together

That was a lot of information to remember. Here is a checklist for you to use whenever you have a presentation to help you remember all the things you have learnt and put your skills to use!

Presentation checklist. Have you:

- [ ] Found out all the necessary details about the location, timing, and format of the presentation?
- [ ] Read the assessment criteria so you are sure about what to include?
- [ ] Made a plan – in whatever way works for you – about what to include, and in which order?
- [ ] Done any relevant research so you have the necessary information or facts you want to include?
- [ ] Made a visual support, such as a slideshow, if required?
- [ ] Created cue cards or notes to help you remember what to say for each section?
- [ ] Rehearsed your presentation?
- [ ] Focused on the positives? Presentations can be scary. Well done for giving it a go. Note what you've done well, or improved at.

GROUP WORK

> "There's a lot of group work on my course. It's okay working with people who I get on with."

During your studies you might be required to complete some assignments as a group. These might be oral presentations, but could also be research projects, written assignments or practical work.

Group work can have many benefits:

- an opportunity to share ideas
- a chance to work with others, get to know other students and work differently
- an opportunity to look at ideas from different perspectives and backgrounds
- practice in giving and receiving peer feedback
- a chance to work on a bigger project than you would be able to do individually
- an opportunity for individual students to work to their strengths and allow other students to help them in areas they find more difficult.

However, there can also be some difficulties and disadvantages:

- Group members might not communicate effectively, leaving people not knowing what to do or redoing work that has been done by others.
- Group members might prefer to work in different, conflicting ways. For example, some might want a structured approach, whereas others will work more spontaneously.

- Some group members might do more of the work than others.
- Some individuals might be less confident communicating within a group.
- There can be frustrations if the group does not agree on what to do or how to approach the work.

> "I felt I did more of the research and organizing than anyone else in the group, but when it came to present our work, I wasn't as confident, so only said a short part, then ended up getting a much lower grade than the other group members. It wasn't fair."

What about you? What have been your experiences of group work?

....
....
....
....
....

You might have had both positive and negative experiences in the past. Perhaps there were times you enjoyed working with others and other times you didn't. Maybe it depended on who the others were in the group, what the task was, or how precise the instructions or expectations were.

> "I find group work difficult. I just want to get on with it and get frustrated when others haven't started or when nobody can agree on what to do or when they don't sense the urgency of the task like I do. It makes me anxious and I worry about it."

What skills do you feel you bring to group work? (E.g. good at listening to others, good at leading and organizing the group, always completing your part of the task on time.)

....
....
....
....
....

Do you have any specific difficulties when working in a group? (E.g. finding the dynamics of group conversation difficult, feeling you let others down by being disorganized.)

....
....
....
....
....

Managing group work

> "I hate group work. Others never seem to take my thoughts on board. I'm not listened to."

Whether group work is something you love or you hate, there are some things that can make it easier. Read the following list and consider if anything might be worth trying for you.

- If you're confident enough, being honest about your individual needs to other group members can be helpful in increasing their understanding. (E.g. "Due to my auditory processing difficulties, I find it hard to remember what has been discussed, so can we write down the list of actions?" or "I know I often misunderstand the question, so can somebody check I'm on the right track with my part before I go too far into it?".)

- Consider at the beginning how you are going to split the work up. It can often be easier for each person to have a specific task to work on.
- Consider also if specific roles are needed for the group task. (E.g. somebody to "chair" the discussions, somebody who'll take notes and share these afterwards, somebody who'll be "timekeeper" and remind others of upcoming deadlines or of when it's time to move on.)
- At group meetings, or online chats, come up with mini-deadlines for actions. This can help the group stay on track and is especially important if one person's work depends on another person completing their part first.
- Make sure that everyone gets to share their thoughts and opinions. Ask group members who have not yet said anything if there's something they would like to add.
- Be honest with group members if you're having problems completing your part, and encourage others to be honest too by remembering to check in.
  - Part of group work is helping each other and dealing with difficulties as a team.
- Consider if coming up with some "group rules" or "group work guidelines" at the beginning of your project might be helpful.
- Ensure each group member is given an equal amount of work to do.
- Allow each individual to work to their strengths.
  - See which parts of the work each person would prefer to do or prefer not to do.
  - Some group members might not be confident, for example, asking people to complete a survey by themselves, but would be able to do this when working with another person.

- Encourage group members to be open about their strengths and difficulties and to suggest solutions.

- Accept that others work in their own way too. A frustration of group work can be if others do not complete their part of the task to the standard you would, or if they do something wildly different than you would.

- Give constructive feedback to group members. Accept constructive feedback from others.

> "I dislike group work. I don't know anyone on my course, so they all get themselves into groups, and it's really awkward having to approach people I don't know and joining in when they are already good friends."

SUMMARY

In this chapter you've learned:

- Effective presentations are usually well-structured and easy-to-follow with relevant visuals. Presenters who are confident being themselves and enthusiastic about their subject are often effective.

- Many people feel anxious about public speaking, but it is a skill that many learn to improve at.

- Planning, structuring and research are just as important for presentations as for written assignments.

- Rehearsing a presentation can help you improve your confidence.

- Various strategies can help you cope with nerves before and during a presentation. If you are particularly anxious about giving a presentation, speak to your tutors about your needs and discuss what support would be helpful.

Chapter 8

REVISION AND EXAMS

In this chapter, we're going to delve into the world of revision and exams. You'll reflect on what you already do well, identify any limiting beliefs or barriers you face, and will develop an insight into effective strategies that will work for you. The chapter starts by focusing on revision strategies before turning to exam technique.

REVISION

So, first of all, what's meant by revision?

You're probably already familiar with the concept of revision – revising what you've already learned, often in preparation for an upcoming test or exam. Revision is a specific study skill which involves revisiting previously learned information and refreshing your knowledge and understanding. You'll probably also be practising how to apply this information to a specific style of exam question, for example you might be required to write a longer essay, answer shorter questions, complete a multiple choice quiz, or analyse a case study.

Why is revision important?

Going over what you've already learned might not sound like the most fun activity, but it can be important if you have an exam coming up. It might have been quite a while since you covered a topic in class and, even if you have a good memory, you're likely to have forgotten some of the details, or not be able to remember everything accurately. Many courses also build on each topic as you go along, so a topic you covered early in the course might be easier to understand once you've covered subsequent topics. Additionally, revising well can help you feel more confident and less anxious about going into the exam. If you know you've been over the work recently and understood it, you'll feel more able to cope.

Where are you now?

Let's start by reflecting on what you currently do when you revise. As you answer the following questions, try to state the facts rather than judging yourself.

How do you currently revise? What do you do? Read, make notes, use AI to generate revision tasks, study with friends...

....
....
....

When, or how often, do you currently revise? The morning of the exam, the evening before, in shorter sessions over a longer period, in one marathon all-nighter...

....
....
....

What goes well? What, if anything, do you find currently works for you? Is a particular strategy more effective than others?

....
....
....
....
....

REVISION AND EXAMS

What have you tried that has not been successful? Can you identify why this didn't work for you? E.g. have you made a wonderful colour-coded revision timetable but then put it away and didn't refer to it again? Have you tried to revise with friends but just ended up chatting?...

....
....
....
....
....

Has there been a time you've revised successfully? Why do you think this was? E.g. you revised well for your driving theory test because you were very motivated to pass...

....
....
....
....

What are your beliefs about your ability to revise and do well in exams? E.g. "I can't focus, so what's the point even trying to revise?", "It makes no difference whether I revise or not", "I get too stressed to do well in exams", "I always misunderstand the questions", "I do well enough without revising"...

....
....
....
....
....

REVISION, EXAMS AND NEURODIVERGENCE

You've probably already got some ideas about how your neurodivergence affects your revision. If you're not yet so clear about what your difficulties are when revising, take a look at the next double spread of some of the common issues for neurodivergent students and see if any resonate with you. Highlight, circle or just remember which sound most like you.

> **Note!** As always, many of these traits are found in the general population too, but neurodivergent individuals are likely to be affected to a greater extent and, in combination with other neurodivergent traits, the impact on functioning is likely to be greater.

Are you like Katie?

If this resonates with you, then the underlying issue might not be with revision but with learning and understanding. It's tricky to revise and remember something you didn't understand originally! Try to seek support as soon as you realize you don't understand something. Leaving it until exam time will be too late.

If you're at school or college, speak to your SENCo or subject tutors. If you're a university student, contact your course tutors or attend their office hours or revision sessions. If you miss any lectures or classes, see if notes or recordings are available. Rewatch any lectures that have been recorded and are accessible on your university's VLE. If you're still having difficulty understanding the content of a course, your college or university's Student Services might be able to point you to useful support – this might be in the form of a mentor, tutor or access to workshops on academic skills.

Are you like Justin, Ali, Jill, Hassan, Anna or Bea?

If any of these sound like you, difficulties with revision might stem from your differences with time management, time perception, organization or focus. Go back to Chapter 4 for a reminder of your individual difficulties and for some useful strategies that you might be able to apply when revising.

Does Thomas sound like you?

First of all, don't despair! Even the process of having sat down and making a revision timetable will have been useful, even if you haven't stuck to it! You've likely spent time looking through your notes and familiarizing yourself with all the topics you've studied which will help you feel more prepared and organized. You also should celebrate your planning and organizational skills.

You just need to consider what happens for you. Is it an issue with focus and concentration? (Again, refer back to Chapter 4 for some ideas.) Do you not factor in enough time for unexpected events in your plan? Do you feel there's no point continuing as soon as you "fall behind"? Do sensory issues, fluctuating energy levels or other health issues impact you? Do you view the timetable as a "demand" (even though self-imposed)?

Or maybe you sound more like Orla, Leo, Isla, Micah, Luna and Nathan?

Statements such as these suggest that you might not be revising as effectively as you could. Perhaps you just don't know what techniques to use or how to approach the task. It might be that you revise, but don't look at how to apply this knowledge to the exam (also known as "exam technique", which is covered later in this chapter). Consider some of the revision strategies outlined in the next section.

Or perhaps you're more like Emily?

If you are motivated more by starting new tasks and learning new things than you are by going back to what you've already learned, consider how you could apply this self-knowledge to your revision. Re-reading your notes probably isn't going to excite you. How could you make revision feel like a new task? Could you attempt past exam papers and refresh your knowledge as you complete these? Could you put together the information in a new way?

KATIE: "I sit down to revise but find it difficult as I didn't really understand the content the first-time round."

JUSTIN: "I want to revise but just don't seem to fit it in."

JILL: "I've got plenty of time to revise. I'll do it tomorrow / next week…"

ALI: "An exam? What?! I thought I had ages before that came around!"

HASSAN: "I sit down to revise but am never sure what I need to revise or what format the exam will take."

MATT: "I start to revise but get distracted. I start chatting to friends or move to another task. I scroll through social media, or sometimes I just start daydreaming or worrying about something."

ANNA: "I do try to revise but I can never find the relevant revision materials and my notes are all mixed up."

ORLA: "Revision is too boring even to contemplate!"

"I tend to hyperfocus on a small topic and then don't leave enough time for most of what I need to revise." — **BEA**

"I make fantastic revision timetables! I break down the topics and colour code everything. Problem is, I just can't seem to stick to it." — **THOMAS**

"I don't bother. I don't know how to do it properly." — **LEO**

"Revision? That's something to do the night before the exam, isn't it?" — **MICAH**

LUNA: "I do revise but don't think I do it very effectively."

"I think I revise well but I get to an exam and can't answer the questions or apply my knowledge." — **NATHAN**

"I like starting new things rather than going back to what I've done before." — **EMILY**

"I don't see the point in revising. There are times I've revised a lot but it didn't make a difference to my exam results, and times I've not revised but I did well!" — **ISLA**

FINDING JOY IN STUDYING

Maybe there's something else for you?

My neurodivergence affects my ability to revise and do well in exams in the following ways:

....

....

....

....

....

....

....

....

....

....

....

....

....

....

....

....

....

....

....

Limiting beliefs

Before investigating revision strategies and exam techniques in more detail, did you identify any limiting beliefs on the previous page which you feel have a negative impact on your revision or how you manage exams?

If you've identified any limiting beliefs, you might like to try the exercise that follows. If not, skip ahead to the "Preparing to revise" section.

Limiting or negative beliefs can influence your behaviour or actions and result in a vicious cycle of negative beliefs, feelings and actions. Look at the example below:

A limiting / negative belief:
(e.g. I can't focus, so there's no point even trying to revise)

Behaviour / action:
(e.g. I don't spend enough time revising)

Feelings:
(e.g. I feel unprepared for exams, I feel a lack of confidence, I feel frustrated etc)

Result:
(e.g. I don't do as well as I could in exams)

Reinforces the belief that...
(e.g. I feel like I can't revise)

FINDING JOY IN STUDYING

 If you discover your own recurring negative beliefs, how do they affect you? Have a go at filling in your own negative beliefs cycle:

**LIMITING BELIEFS
PART A**

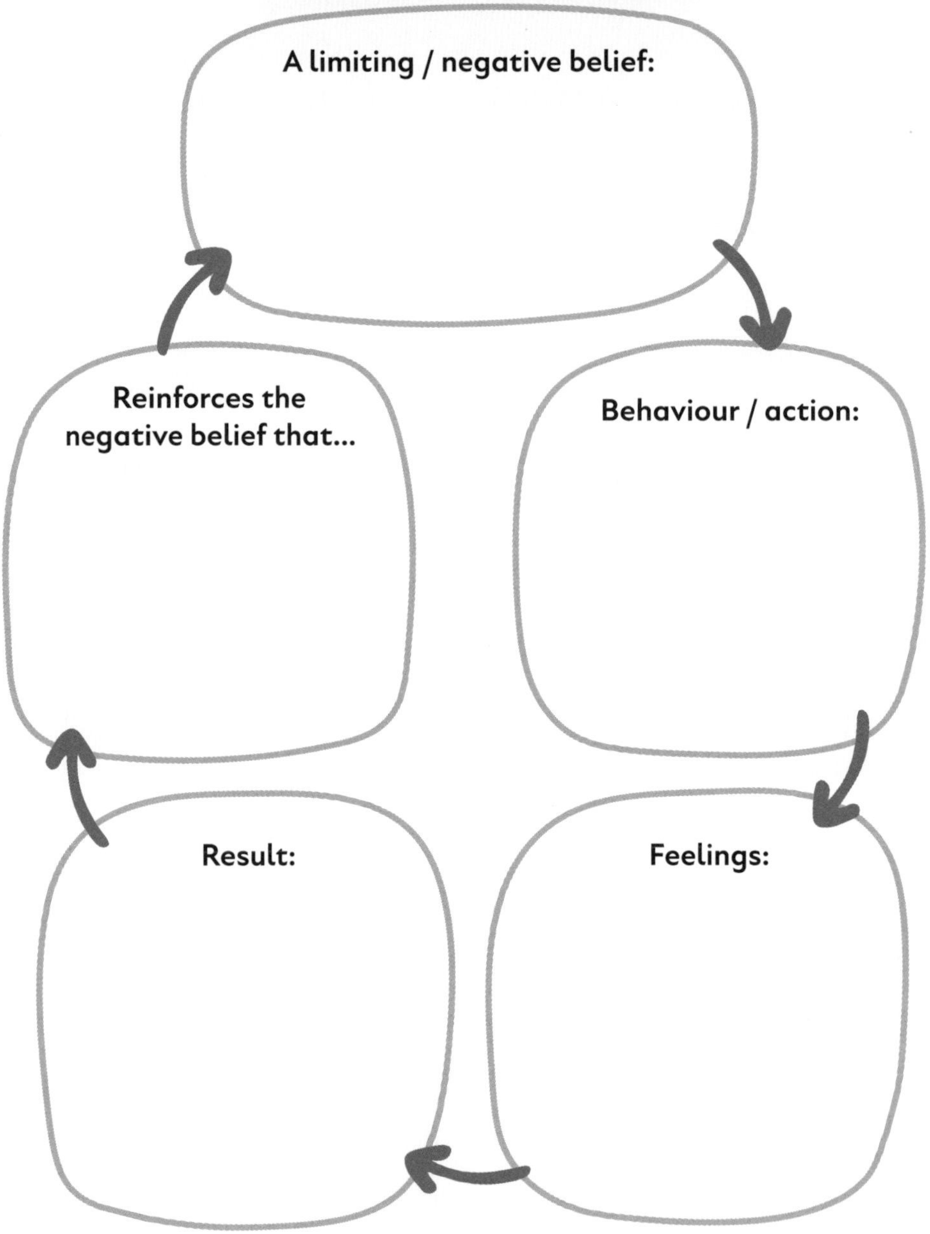

A limiting / negative belief:

Behaviour / action:

Feelings:

Result:

Reinforces the negative belief that...

You might not find it easy to recognize any limiting beliefs. You could also consider any unhelpful behaviours or actions relating to revision and exams. Start filling in the cycle from the "Behaviour / action" box instead and see if that helps you identify what the limiting belief behind your actions is.

Now, just because you believe something, that doesn't mean it's true. For thousands of years, humans believed the Earth was flat, but that didn't mean it actually was! It's now time to try challenging your belief. What might be a more objective thought?

Let's look at an example.

Original belief

(e.g. I find revision so boring. There's no point in me doing it as I'll get bored too quickly and give up)

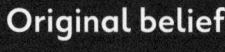

Challenged belief

(e.g. It's worth me revising, even for ten minutes at a time. All those ten minutes will add up, and I can learn strategies that will work to help make revision more interesting for me)

FINDING JOY IN STUDYING

 Challenging your beliefs isn't about denying your neurodivergent differences or health conditions. It's about accepting your individual profile, referring to your strengths (e.g. a willingness to try out new strategies) and considering the issue objectively. Try to challenge your own beliefs this way:

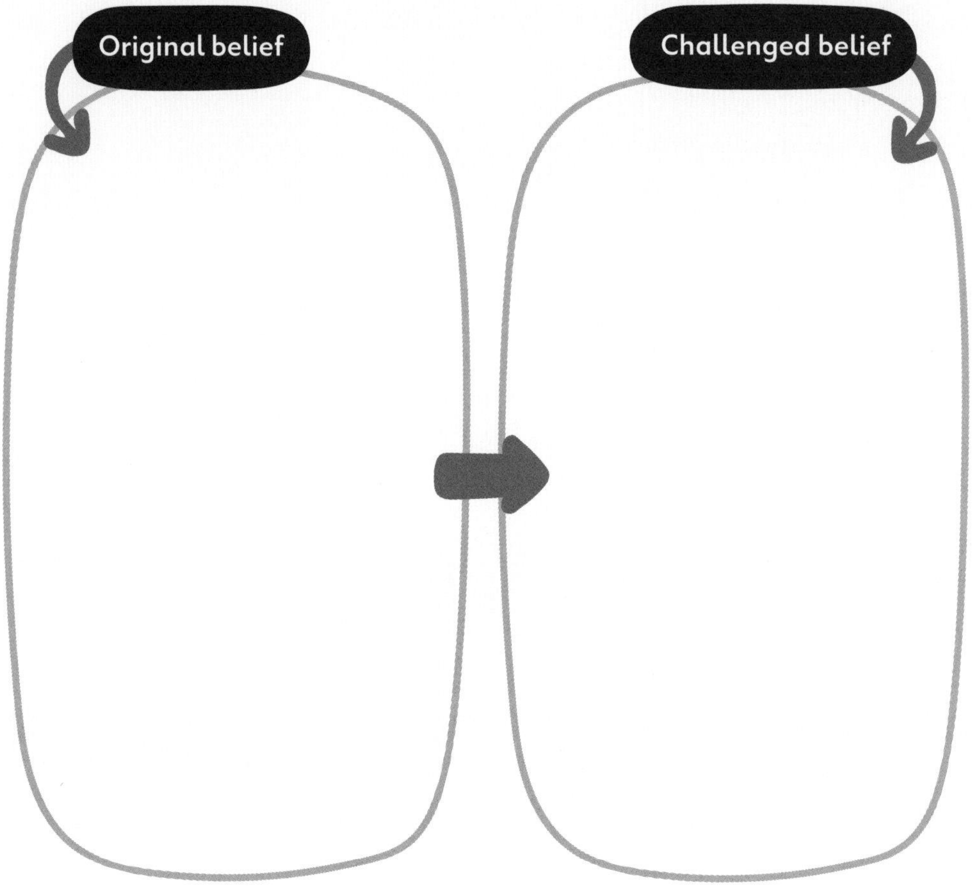

Original belief

Challenged belief

REVISION AND EXAMS

Now imagine the effect this new belief will have on your cycle of thoughts, feelings and actions:

New belief:
(e.g. I can find it hard to focus, but I can learn strategies that work for me and it's still worth revising in short bursts)

Behaviour / action:
(e.g. I revise in short bursts using strategies that work for me)

Feelings:
(e.g. I feel more prepared for exams, I feel an increase of confidence, I feel less frustrated etc)

Result:
(e.g. I do better in exams than previously)

Reinforces the belief that...
(e.g. I CAN revise – I just need to learn strategies to do it in my own way)

FINDING JOY IN STUDYING

 Using your new belief, how will the cycle change for you?

LIMITING BELIEFS
PART B

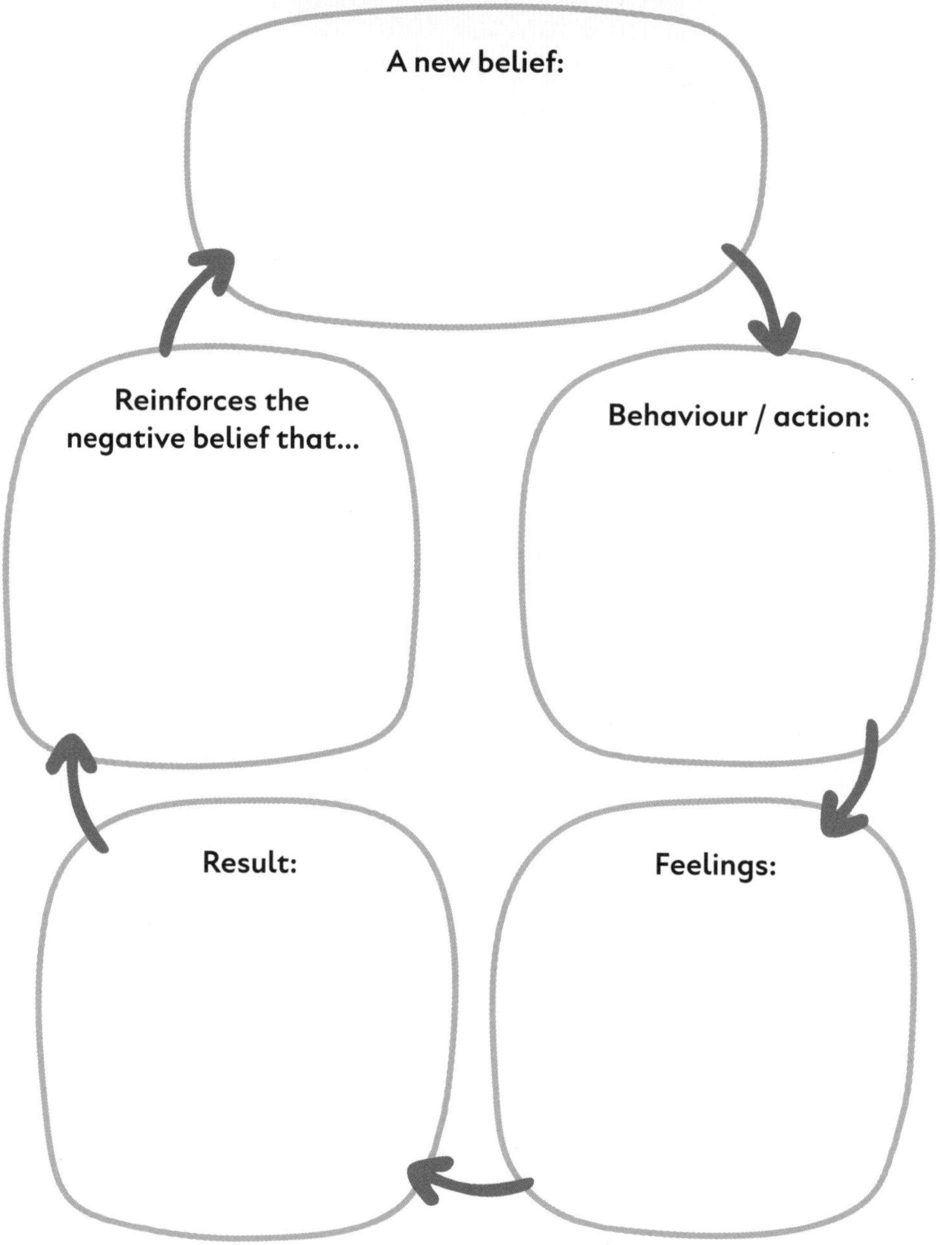

A new belief:

Reinforces the negative belief that...

Behaviour / action:

Result:

Feelings:

Preparing to revise

Before thinking about **how** to revise, you need to know exactly **what** to revise. You might revise really well, but if you've revised the wrong topic or spent ages memorizing quotations that you'll have access to in the exam, then it's time wasted.

Ask yourself the following questions before you start revising:

What subject / module do you need to revise?

....

....

....

....

....

Are you allowed access to any resources in the exam? (E.g. texts, equation lists.)

....

....

....

....

....

- Refer also to the exam preparation checklist later in this chapter.

Revision strategies

There's no single way to revise that's guaranteed to work for everyone. As you've already learned in previous chapters, you really have to find out what works *for you*. Working through this book, you're gaining valuable insights into how your brain works, your individual strengths and difficulties, and any limiting beliefs or patterns of behaviour. This self-knowledge is key to developing more effective revision skills. So, as you read the following information, engage critically with the ideas. Which strategies do you think might work or not work for you? Which do you think you could adapt so they do work for you?

Possible revision strategies

The table below contains some ideas about how to revise. Some strategies might be more suitable for certain subjects than for others.

> **Tip!** The most effective revision strategies are often those that require you to engage with the content actively rather than passively. So, making notes on a text, for example, is more effective than simply reading it.

Make a mind-map. Try making a mind-map of everything you can remember about a topic. Then look up the content you are less confident on.	**Use your notes.** Re-read your course notes. Try highlighting key points or transferring key information into a mind-map or diagram.
Watch and listen. Watch revision videos or listen to relevant podcasts and note the key points.	**Test yourself.** Doing online quizzes, or answering questions from revision books, can help identify areas of strength and areas you need to revisit.
Do past papers. Ask your tutor or teacher for past exam papers. Have a go and then compare your answers to the mark scheme.	**Make revision cards.** Write a question on one side and the answer on the other. Use these to test yourself or ask a friend to test you.
Teach somebody. Teach a friend or family member about a topic you have revised. Encourage them to ask you questions and to tell you when they need you to explain something.	**Put the information into a different format.** Can you create a comic strip, flow diagram, story, song or poem about a topic?
Use your classmates. Study with classmates. Test or teach each other using as many different strategies as possible.	**Use strategies to jog your memory.** Mnemonics can be useful for some people (e.g. *Richard Of York Gave Battle In Vain* gives the order of the rainbow colours – Red, Orange, Yellow, Green, Blue, Indigo, Violet).
Two minutes. Try to talk for two minutes about a topic with no hesitations or repetitions. This can identify topics you know well or need to revisit.	**Top ten.** Choose a topic. Can you select the ten most important facts about that topic? Make a note of them. Why do you think these are most important?

REVISION AND EXAMS

Match it up. Make small cards (or sticky notes) with key words. Write their definitions on a separate card. Can you match them up accurately in your next revision session?	**Identify gaps.** Read through your class notes. Highlight anything you don't understand. How could you work on these topics? (Read, research, ask your tutor, ask a classmate...)
Read and recall. Read a page of a revision guide or textbook. Close it. Now try to note down or make a voice memo of everything you can remember using your own words. Then open the book and identify what you missed.	**Make it fun.** Consider how you can turn revision into fun games, quizzes or activities.

A REVISION PLAN

Which of the above strategies are you going to try out?

....
....
....
....
....
....
....

Are there any strategies you want to try but think you need to adapt? How will you adapt them so they suit you better?

....
....
....
....
....
....
....

Do any strategies lend themselves more effectively to certain topics? Try making a list of topics you need to revise and note down a suitable revision strategy for that topic.

Topic:	Possible strategy to try for this:

Timetabling the revision

Once you're sure on **what** you need to revise and have ideas of **how** to revise it, you need to consider **when** you're going to try and get this done. You might decide to create a revision timetable in the lead-up to the exam, engage in ongoing revision, or in some combination of the two.

Revision timetables

Some students like to come up with a revision timetable.

To create a revision timetable:

1. Start by making a list of all the topics you'll need to revise for the exam.

2. Consider the exam date. Find time in your schedule before this to revise each topic. Writing each revision topic and session in your diary or calendar can be helpful to ensure you remember to do the revision. Look back to Chapter 4 for strategies to help with time management and focus.

3. Be realistic about the time needed for each topic and about what works best for you. Do you prefer shorter revision sessions, or longer ones? Will larger topics need to be split up across several sessions?

4. Remember to factor in "spare sessions" to make up for any times that other things get in the way (e.g. illness, unexpected events).

Ongoing revision

Not everyone finds revision timetables useful. Some might find that difficulties concentrating mean that time isn't used effectively, that other things get in the way, that they feel too pressured to revise at a set time (even if the pressure is self-imposed) or they struggle to feel motivated at the allocated time.

If you think you're unlikely to stick to a revision plan, you could turn back to Chapter 4 to remind yourself about strategies you find useful when it comes to helping you focus and manage your time. Consider what other alternatives there are. If you're not going to stick to a revision plan, how are you going to get the revision done?

Revision doesn't have to be done solely at the end of the term immediately before an exam. It can be an ongoing process and, indeed, it is often more effective to revise little and often, as this will keep the knowledge fresher in your mind, meaning less need for intensive last-minute revision anyway.

- You could ensure revision quizzes or activities are accessible on your phone and, for example, do them when on public transport commuting or at other suitable points in your day. Even just a few minutes here and there can be useful. Set yourself an alarm or reminder on your phone if you'd find this useful.

- Consider your daily habits. Do you, for example, often turn up to lectures ten minutes early? Why not use these ten minutes to recap the learning from the previous week? This ongoing "revision" will help you consolidate your knowledge.

- Link revision into existing habits. What do you do every day? Brush your teeth? Boil the kettle? Why not try making a poster of a topic you need to revise and displaying it above the bathroom sink or near the kettle? Having the information somewhere visible where you stand every day can be a reminder to look at it and think about it.

FINDING JOY IN STUDYING

- Attend revision classes arranged by your school or university when they're put on.

What's your plan? When are you going to revise?

....
....
....
....
....
....
....
....
....
....

Can you schedule this in your diary or calendar so you're more likely to remember?

....
....

What else could help you get the revision done? (Making plans to revise with friends etc.)

....
....
....
....
....

REVISION AND EXAMS

Can you do any of these things right now? (E.g. message friends to arrange a revision sessions, find out when your tutor is putting on revision sessions?)

....
....

And, most importantly, how are you going to make this fun? What do you enjoy doing and how could you link this to revising?

....
....
....
....
....

Focusing and getting the revision done

So far, this chapter has helped you reflect on your current revision strategies, identify more effective ways to revise and has encouraged you to plan effectively. Hopefully, you're now in a much better position to make the best use of your time and revise confidently and effectively. However, actually getting the revision done is the most important thing.

- Flick back to Chapter 4: "Time Management, Focus and Organization" to remind yourself what works for you.

- Sometimes "Just Doing It" might be beneficial. Often, thinking about revision is much more stressful than actually doing it! Once you get started, the task might start to seem less overwhelming.

- Identify your motivators. Does working with a study buddy help? Working in a library with fewer distractions?

What will help you focus and concentrate when revising?

EXAMS

Let's consider now the exams themselves.

How do you feel before exams?

....
....
....
....
....

How about afterwards?

....
....
....
....
....

What strategies do you usually use in exams? (E.g. doing easier questions first, doing shorter questions first, reading through the whole exam paper first?)

....
....
....
....
....

REVISION AND EXAMS

What do you find most difficult in the exam situation?

....
....
....
....
....
....
....
....
....
....

What have you learned about yourself? Do you stress about exams but actually do okay in them? If that's the case, you'll probably benefit from focusing on ways to reduce nerves. Do you find it difficult to manage your time in exams and spend too long on one question before having to rush the others? Or are there other things that you find difficult?

Students often experience difficulties such as:

- feeling stressed in the run-up to an exam
- feeling nervous during the exam itself and therefore not being able to think as clearly as they could usually
- mis-reading the instructions
- mis-reading the questions
- not allocating their time appropriately between the questions
- not giving the right amount of information in their answers
- not knowing what the question is asking.

In addition, some neurodivergent students experience specific difficulties when taking exams. These might include:

- being overwhelmed with anxiety before or during an exam
- finding a physical exam hall overwhelming due to sensory sensitivities
- needing more processing time to understand written or aural information than is given in an exam
- finding it difficult to concentrate for the length of an exam
- having difficulty in interpreting what the question is asking or "reading between the lines"
- difficulties managing time and focus within an exam
- worrying excessively before and after an exam about the results
- slow handwriting speed which impacts on written exams.

Exam access arrangements

Some of these difficulties and differences might be reduced with exam access arrangements. If you're eligible for these, you might be granted concessions such as:

- extra time to complete an exam
- rest breaks in an exam
- a separate room to complete the exam in
- the use of technology which will allow you to have questions read aloud or type your answers instead of handwriting them.

You will need to be assessed for these concessions. If you haven't already been assessed and think you might be eligible, it's important to speak to your SENCo or Disability Advisor as soon as possible, so this process can be started. If you leave it too close to your exams, you might not receive any concessions in time. It's also important to ensure that any concessions you are given actually work for you. If you are given specialist software to use, for example, make sure you've been shown how to use it in advance.

Consider carefully what your needs are and discuss your options with your SENCo or Disability Advisor.

Exam technique

Do you know what exam technique is?

Effective exam technique can make a huge difference to how well you do in exams. Exam technique is about being able to apply your knowledge to the exam situation and managing your time well in the exam. Some exams, such as practical exams, oral exams or computer-based exams, might have specific instructions, but here are some general pointers you might have identified that are relevant in most exam situations:

Be prepared
Ensure you know which topics are covered in which exams, what format the exam will take, what resources you are allowed and what you need to take.

Check which questions you need to answer
Sometimes instructions state "Answer Question 1 **OR** Question 2". Miss this and you'll waste time answering two questions, one of which won't be marked.

Divide your time appropriately
Check how many marks are awarded for each question. If you have an hour to answer two questions each worth ten marks, spend roughly half the time on each one. If one question is worth five marks and the second worth 15, then you know to spend a much shorter time on the first question.

Read the instructions VERY carefully
It can be easy to miss things when you're feeling anxious in an exam. Take a few deep breaths and read the instructions slowly. Do exactly what it tells you to do (e.g. "Include quotations", "Circle the correct response", "Answer Question 3 OR Question 4").

Answer the question
Look back at the "Written Assignments" chapter in this book for guidance. Ensure you are answering what the question is asking, that your answer is

relevant and that you are responding to the correct command (e.g. is the question asking you to "describe", "explain", "analyse", "compare"?).

Work in a way that suits you
Often you don't have to complete the questions in a set order. Some people prefer to do the ones they're more confident about first, and then go back to those they need to think harder about.

Have a go
Even if you're not sure, have a go at answering every question. You won't get any marks for leaving something out, but might get some for having a go.

What about you? Is there anything you think you need to try out in future exams to improve your performance?

....
....
....
....
....
....
....
....
....

How could you get support with this? (E.g. would it help to complete some past exam papers for your subject in "mock exam" conditions? Do you need to revise question command words?)

....
....
....
....

REVISION AND EXAMS

. . . .
. . . .
. . . .
. . . .
. . . .

Being prepared for an exam can help you revise more effectively and feel less overwhelmed on exam day. Try completing the following exam preparation checklist for each exam you have coming up. If you can't answer any of the questions, try to find the answers as soon as you can.

EXAM 1

Exam subject:	
Date:	
Time:	
Length:	
Location:	
Topics covered in this exam:	
Format (e.g. multiple choice, long essays, short answer, paper-based, computer-based):	
Resources you need to take:	
Resources provided:	

EXAM 2

Exam subject:	
Date:	
Time:	
Length:	
Location:	
Topics covered in this exam:	
Format (e.g. multiple choice, long essays, short answer, paper-based, computer-based):	
Resources you need to take:	
Resources provided:	

EXAM 3

Exam subject:	
Date:	
Time:	
Length:	
Location:	
Topics covered in this exam:	

Format (e.g. multiple choice, long essays, short answer, paper-based, computer-based):	
Resources you need to take:	
Resources provided:	

EXAM 4

Exam subject:	
Date:	
Time:	
Length:	
Location:	
Topics covered in this exam:	
Format (e.g. multiple choice, long essays, short answer, paper-based, computer-based):	
Resources you need to take:	
Resources provided:	

EXAM 5

Exam subject:	
Date:	
Time:	
Length:	
Location:	
Topics covered in this exam:	
Format (e.g. multiple choice, long essays, short answer, paper-based, computer-based):	
Resources you need to take:	
Resources provided:	

Coping with exam stress

How stressful do you find exam time?

....

....

....

....

What has helped you cope in the past?

. . . .

. . . .

. . . .

. . . .

Coping with exams can be stressful. You might worry that you're not doing enough revision or don't feel prepared enough. You might find the worry stops you revising as effectively as you could or you might be so nervous in the actual exam that you can't show your knowledge as well as you know you could at other times. You might worry excessively after completing an exam and find the months waiting for the results are agonizing. A little bit of stress can sometimes be helpful – feeling a little stressed about an upcoming exam, for example, might motivate you to do some revision and preparation – but feeling overwhelmed by stress isn't helpful. You might already have some ideas about what helps you to cope with times of stress and overwhelm. If you do, try to ensure that you schedule time for activities or strategies that you know are beneficial. If you're not sure what could help, you could consider some of the following ideas.

Stress-busting hobbies
Making time for hobbies that help you feel relaxed can be particularly important during exam season. Walking, running, exercise classes, going to the gym, reading, crafting, watching your favourite television shows – whatever it is that helps you.

Spend time outdoors
Research (Coventry et al., 2021) suggests that spending time outdoors in nature can help to reduce anxiety. Maybe you could seek out green spaces for a walk, picnic or to meet friends? Spending some time gardening, walking the dog or simply relaxing outside could also be helpful.

Talk it through

Sometimes, talking about your worries with friends or family members can help you manage. Keeping up social connections and contacts can also be helpful during revision time to combat feelings of isolation and overwhelm.

Meditation, mindfulness and yoga

Many students find activities such as meditation and mindfulness helpful to reduce feelings of stress and overwhelm. These activities can take many forms – guided meditations, mindfulness techniques, yoga, visualizations or breathwork, for example – and you might have to try out several activities to find which suits you best. Every teacher will also teach these activities in a different style and use different techniques, so it's worth trying out a few different classes or groups. When choosing a class, consider your neurodiversity and any other health needs. Do you prefer a face-to-face class or online? A live class or watching / listening to a recording? Do you find it hard to visualize? A class with lots of visualizations might not work for you. Do you have heightened sensory sensitivities? Paying close attention to sounds might not be relaxing for you. If you have difficulties breathing or have panic attacks, a focus on breathwork might not be calming for you. Experienced teachers should be able to offer alternatives and will take individual needs into account.

Put it into perspective

During exam time, the stress might feel all-important and all-consuming. Sometimes it can be helpful to remind yourself that exam time won't go on forever. Simply reminding yourself that "this too will pass" and that your exams will be over in a couple of weeks can be helpful. Remind yourself too that exams are often only part of your final marks – many courses combine exam results with coursework results or practical elements. If you find affirmations helpful, you could create some for the exam period:

- "This stressful time will pass."
- "I will do the best I can and that is enough."
- "I have worked hard."

Be kind and non-judgemental

Worrying about exams once you've completed them won't change your marks. If you find your thoughts dwelling on answers you should have written or improvements you could have made, try to catch these thoughts before you engage with them. Be kind and non-judgemental to yourself. Maybe you could smile and say to yourself, "Okay, hey there mind, you are worrying about that exam you did again! You really do like to think about it, don't you? But it's done now. Going over it again won't change anything. Let's focus on something else now." Gently try to bring your attention back to something in the here and now.

Negative cognitive bias

Psychologists recognize a phenomenon called "negative cognitive bias". As humans, we've evolved to tend to notice and remember the "negatives" rather than the positives, even if the positives outnumber the negatives. For our ancestors, noticing bad or dangerous threats in the world would have been quite literally a matter of life or death. In the modern world, it's probably not quite so helpful. But it's useful to recognize that this is often how our minds work. You might be worrying about the one question you couldn't answer in an exam, and totally forget that there were five other questions that you answered very confidently. If you notice yourself dwelling on the negatives, make a conscious effort to think of the positives too.

Remember – You're not alone

If you find revision and exams stressful, you are certainly not alone! They are stressful times for a lot of people, and sometimes reminding yourself of this can be useful. If you chat to classmates and friends, you'll likely find that many are feeling some sort of stress or anxiety during exam time.

Seek support

Some of the strategies above might be enough to help you cope during revision and exam season, but there might be times you need more support. If you have a mentor, you might speak to them. Most colleges and universities have counselling and wellbeing services available. Help is also available through your GP, health services and various charities. Helplines such as the Samaritans are also accessible to all.

It's never as bad as it seems

Many people find that they actually do much better than they expected in exams. Sometimes, however, there might be times when you don't do as well as you'd hoped and it can be easy to feel down about this and worry about the implications. Some people jump to the conclusion that doing badly in exams will have a negative impact on the rest of their lives. In reality, this isn't the case at all! If your results aren't as good as you hoped, there are likely to be many options open to you. Sometimes, there is the option to simply retake the exam at a later date, or possibly retake the module or year if needed. Often, even if you obtain a lower result than expected, your results will still be good enough to get you on to the course, training or job you were planning on moving on to. Employers and training providers look for more than exam results – your work experience, other experiences and skills will all be taken into account. And often, there are many alternative routes into different professions. Remind yourself that there are always back-up plans, and not quite getting the grades you wanted – although it can seem huge at the time – isn't always significant in the longer term.

Exam action plan

Now you've researched your upcoming exams, reflected on past exams you've taken and have completed your revision and / or any past exam papers, what is your plan for the real exams? Bullet list the most important strategies you want to keep in mind (e.g. "Highlight the key words in each question", "Take a few slow breaths to calm my nerves, then read through the instructions twice", "Not spend too long worrying about questions I think are difficult – do the others first, then come back to these"...).

I'm going to...

- ....
- ....
- ....
- ....
- ....
- ....

SUMMARY

In this chapter you've learned:

- Revision includes going over the content of what you've learned, as well as learning how to apply this to the exam situation.

- Revision requires effective time management, organization and focus (return to Chapter 4 for ideas).

- "Active" learning strategies are usually more effective than reading or listening passively.

- Find revision strategies that appeal to you. What do you find fun and engaging? Work with your natural inclinations too – when do you feel most focused and energized?

- Effective exam technique can make a big difference to how you do in exams. A little preparation and practice can go a long way.

Congratulations for reaching the end of this book! Remember as you grow and change, you can come back as many times as you need to – and you can reuse your downloadable resources over and over again too, no matter what you're studying. I hope you, like me, through getting to know yourself, have found the joy in studying!

Further Resources

ADHD UK – UK charity with informative webpage about ADHD: www.adhduk.co.uk

British Dyslexia Association – UK charity with informative webpage about dyslexia and dyscalculia: www.bdadyslexia.org.uk

Kooth – UK service providing mental health and wellbeing support to young people: www.kooth.com

Mind – UK charity with an informative website about all aspects of mental health. Information also about local branches of Mind throughout the UK: www.mind.org.uk

National Autistic Society – UK charity with informative website about autism: www.autism.org.uk

NHS – Information pages from the NHS about dyspraxia / DCD: www.nhs.uk/conditions/developmental-coordination-disorder-dyspraxia

Prospects – UK website about graduate jobs and careers: www.prospects.ac.uk

The Complete University Guide – UK website which includes a course search and guidance about university life: www.thecompleteuniversityguide.co.uk

UCAS – UK organization through which applications to undergraduate courses are made. A website about university life and courses on offer: www.ucas.com

Young Minds – UK charity focusing on young people's mental health and wellbeing: www.youngminds.org.uk.

References

ADHD UK (2024) 'About ADHD.' Accessed 21 February 2024 at https://adhduk.co.uk/about-adhd.
Attwood, T. & Garnett, M. (2022) 'What is autistic burnout?' Accessed 22 February 2024 at www.attwoodandgarnettevents.com/what-is-autistic-burnout.
BDA (British Dyslexia Association) (2024a) 'About dyslexia.' Accessed 21 February 2024 at www.bdadyslexia.org.uk/dyslexia/about-dyslexia/signs-of-dyslexia.
BDA (British Dyslexia Association) (2024b) 'About dyscalculia.' Accessed 21 February 2024 at www.bdadyslexia.org.uk/dyscalculia/how-can-i-identify-dyscalculia.
Clinton, V. (2019) 'Reading from paper compared to screens: A systematic review and meta-analysis.' *Journal of Research in Reading, 42*, 2. https://doi.org/10.1111/1467-9817.12269
Coventry, P.A., Brown, J.V.E., Pervin, J., Braybn, S. et al. (2021) 'Nature-based outdoor activities for mental and physical health: Systematic review and meta-analysis.' *SSM – Population Health, 16*, 100934.
Donaghy, B., Moore, D. & Green, J. (2023) 'Co-occurring physical health challenges in neurodivergent children and young people: A topical review and recommendation.' *Child Care in Practice, 29*, 1, 3–21, DOI: 10.1080/13575279.2022.2149471
Foundation for People with Learning Disabilities (2024) 'Dyspraxia.' Accessed 11 October 2024 at www.learningdisabilities.org.uk/learning-disabilities/a-to-z/d/dyspraxia.
Kenny, L., Hattersley, C., Molins, B., Buckley, C., Povey, C. & Pellicano, E. (2015) 'Which terms should be used to describe autism? Perspectives from the UK autism community.' *Autism, 20*, 4, 442–462. https://doi.org/10.1177/1362361315588200
May, K.E. & Elder, A.D. (2018) 'Efficient, helpful, or distracting? A literature review of media multitasking in relation to academic performance.' *International Journal of Educational Technology in Higher Education, 15*, 13. https://doi.org/10.1186/s41239-018-0096-z
NAS (National Autistic Society) (2022) 'Understanding autistic burnout.' Accessed 25 March 2024 at www.autism.org.uk/advice-and-guidance/professional-practice/autistic-burnout.
NAS (National Autistic Society) (2024) 'What is autism?' Accessed 21 February 2024 at www.autism.org.uk/advice-and-guidance/what-is-autism.
Obaydi, H. & Puri, B.K. (2008) 'Prevalence of premenstrual syndrome in autism: A prospective observer-rated study.' *Journal of International Medical Research, 36*, 2, 268–272. https://doi.org/10.1177/147323000803600208